Education in a Violent World

Education in a Violent World

A Practical Guide to Keeping Our Kids Safe

Dr. Steven Webb

Prominent Books

Editing: Writer Services, LLC (WriterServices.net)
Cover Design & Book Layout: Writer Services, LLC

ISBN-10: 1-942389-23-X
ISBN-13: 978-1-942389-23-1

Prominent Books and the Prominent Books logo are Trademarks of Prominent Books, LLC

TABLE OF CONTENTS

ACKNOWLEDGMENTS

To sit down and create a book, a guide to help save children's lives no less, takes an immense toll on emotions and passions. Although this book uses words from my heart, I find myself speechless when I think about the contributions of so many people who helped shape my life and my purpose for living and wanting to make a difference.

First, to my parents and grandparents who have all passed now but who didn't just teach me the difference between right and wrong; they showed it in their desire and compassion.

My dad, Bob, was a teacher, a coach, and a school administrator before me, as I am now. He fought many battles but lost to cancer. But before he died, he showed the world why being a teacher is much more than teaching. The line at his visitation was so long with former students, we added an additional visitation to accommodate those who came to see him one last time. That is a teacher, and that is how you shape the world, and that is why I am who and what I am today.

To my wife and high school sweetheart, Angie, and my kids who deal with my constant need to always "have a plan." You were my best plan, and I cannot adequately put into words what you mean to me. I love you all so much.

To my hometown of Goreville, Illinois and the Goreville Community Unit School District #1, who pushed me to spread the word and supported me and my quest to not just help our community but every child in the world. I thank you and have and will always work to make you proud because I am so proud of you (#BlackcatPride). There are countless others who have worked with me, cried with me, and fought by my side. I will never forget where I came from and the impact you have made on my life and mission. We are all in this together for a better world.

INTRODUCTION

"We are now faced with the fact that tomorrow is today. We are confronted with the fierce urgency of now. In this unfolding conundrum of life and history, there 'is' such a thing as being too late. This is no time for apathy or complacency. This is a time for vigorous and positive action."

—Martin Luther King, Jr.

These words, delivered before a gathering of clergy on April 4, 1967, were filled with the impassioned sense of exigency the country had come to expect from Dr. King. It was as if he knew his own time on earth would be limited, and indeed, exactly one year to the day from that speech, he would be killed by an assassin's bullet on the balcony of a Memphis hotel. The sentiment expressed above, however, was much more far reaching than even he could have anticipated. In fact, it was eerily prescient of the culture of complacency we live in today.

Complacency is defined by Merriam-Webster as "self-satisfaction, especially when accompanied by unawareness of actual dangers or deficiencies."

In many ways, we are more hyper-aware than ever before.

We worry about everything from trans fat to terrorism, fracking to fake news, yet we have never been more complacent. It is almost as if we believe that by blogging and tweeting about an issue, we've somehow done our part to deal with it. Unfortunately, nothing could be further from the truth, and nowhere is this inefficiency more apparent and devastating than in the way we treat our children.

In Littleton, Colorado, there is a memorial site for the twelve people killed and twenty-one injured on April 20, 1999, the day that Eric Harris and Dylan Klebold attacked their high school with handguns, sawed-off shotguns, and ninety-nine improvised explosive devices. A plaque at the site reads, "It brought the nation to its knees, but now that we've gotten back up, how have things changed; what have we learned?" Sadly, we have not acted on the painful lessons of that event, something that, after decades in education and law enforcement, I can attest to firsthand.

After beginning my career as a teacher, I became a principal and then superintendent. Once we found that it was extremely difficult to employ and retain a quality school resource officer, I entered the police academy and became the school resource officer of a small rural school district in Illinois—one of just a handful of school administrators who are also law enforcement officers in the nation. I have the honor of helping bring out the best not only in children but also in the faculty who devote their lives to serving the next generation. As a member of the child death review team for the state's Department of Children and Family Services, I have seen the disturbing results of worst-case scenarios.

Each day, kids walk into school facing a litany of physical, emotional and intellectual threats that just fifteen years ago were unimaginable. Whereas they used to be apprehensive of that bully on the playground, now, thanks to texting and social media, anyone can find themselves on the wrong end of a relentless, twenty-four-seven campaign of terror. Rumors are no longer just whispered in the school hallways but posted, retweeted and shared over Snapchat or whatever the newest social platform might be, leaving its victims completely vulnerable, with no refuge.

Violence also exists for today's children at an unprecedented level. Not only are they subjected to the predominately negative twenty-four-hour news cycle, but they live in fear that their school will be the site of the next mass shooting, machete attack or bombing.

Individuality is also under attack. Children are expected to conform to arbitrary norms and follow a homogenized "path to success." Those who do not live up to these standards face harsh penalties. Whereas a small percentage of "unruly" kids used to be diagnosed with a mental condition, today, increasing numbers of children are being slapped with labels like ADHD and Oppositional Defiant Disorder and are medicated—sometimes for years—with harmful drugs that cause a plethora of issues worse than the original, and often questionable, diagnosis. Teachers, who are under increasing pressure to deliver high standardized test scores or risk federal and state funding, often embrace this quick fix as a way of managing their classrooms. However, as discussed in later chapters, these drugs have been cited as responsible for the heinous acts of violence we hear about with alarming regularity.

No child is immune to these threats, as they cross racial, religious, socioeconomic and geographical lines. A child growing up in the inner city may be more susceptible to gang violence, while a gender non-conforming child—regardless of where he lives or how much money his parents have—is more likely to be harassed to the point of suicide. No longer can we presume our children are safe because we live within a certain area code or tax bracket. The danger exists largely on a digital plane and has constant access to them through their ever-present cell phones, computers and tablets.

More than ever, our youth need protection and guidance, yet, all too often, it is conspicuously absent. When someone does not take the threat of terrorism seriously, they are accused of living in a "pre-9/11 world." Since that horrific day, we must be wary, not only when we travel on a plane, but when we are at a crowded concert or even eating in a restaurant. We are taught not to live in fear but to be vigilant and prepared for anything. The same is true for the threat of harm to our children. U.S. schools are "soft targets" for violence, susceptible to attack from outsiders and dangerous meltdowns from insiders—and the typical school safety plan does nothing to change that. Those who continue to operate as we did in the days before Facebook existed and when Columbine stood out as one unthinkable, isolated tragedy is to do kids the most egregious harm of all. It robs them of the security every child, regardless of their circumstances, is entitled to.

This book seeks to inform parents, educators and lawmakers of the depth and breadth of the issues facing our children today and to provide practical tools to make our schools into nurturing, inclusive environments that engage and inspire them to be the best version of themselves. It will also explain the PARA Method, which I developed to prevent and respond to violence from predators both inside and outside of the school. PARA, which comprises four overlapping steps—Preparation, Awareness, Response, and Action—encapsulates what I've learned through assessing my own school district and through my consulting practice, Safe School Systems, LLC, which conducts threat assessments, recommends operational practices, and collaborates with schools that want to build a safety culture. The PARA Method is the 21st-century framework for making schools safe.

Ultimately, however, my goal in writing this book is not to plug one particular solution or philosophy but to pierce the culture of complacency plaguing our society, for as another visionary Helen Keller once said, "He who is content with what has been done is an obstacle in the path of progress."

CHAPTER 1
Bullying

"If you turn and face the other way when someone is being bullied, you might as well be the bully too."

—*Unknown*

Ask almost any fan of 80's movies, and they will list *My Bodyguard* among their favorites. With its mix of unknown actors and famous brat packers Matt Dillon and Joan Cusack, the film quickly took its place among such cult classics as *Pretty in Pink* and *The Breakfast Club*. Like those other studies of high school discontent, *My Bodyguard* tackles the social stratification among American students based on socioeconomics, physical appearance and intelligence, yet it is the only film whose primary focus is on bullying. It is the story of Clifford, a wealthy teen who hires another student to protect him from a gang of school bullies headed by Dillon. His new bodyguard Ricky is a physically intimidating and emotionally troubled teen who, according to high school lore, has a history of violence. After a rocky start, Clifford and Ricky become friends, each helping the other work through his demons. At the end of the movie, there is a final showdown with the bullies, and at Ricky's coaching, Clifford punches out one of the thugs, thoroughly vindicating himself, and tying up the story in a neat little bow. As the credits begin to roll, Ricky and Clifford walk off into the sunset, with Ricky joking that maybe Clifford should be his bodyguard. The implication is that Clifford's life has been changed for the better. No one is ever going to victimize him again, and he will go on to be a self-actualized, confident adult. The film's original promo poster reflects this sentiment with quotes like, "*My Bodyguard* is a soul-satisfying film, totally involving and richly rewarding. It touches the heart."

Flash forward to 2017 and the Netflix show *13 Reasons Why*. It is the story of Hannah, a beautiful, intelligent girl brought low by a number of negative experiences, chief among them rape and bullying. Despondent and alone, she sees her well-meaning but overwhelmed school counselor and leaves the session even more convinced that life isn't worth living. She kills herself, but not before making several cassette tapes of her reasons for ending it all. Two weeks after her suicide, the tapes are delivered to a classmate, who embarks on a sort of posthumous advocacy/revenge campaign on her behalf. In the meantime, Hannah's devastated parents, teachers and schoolmates are left trying to figure out what went wrong, what they could have done to save her, and heal the gaping hole in their lives. It is a story of hopelessness and social isolation, and for the bullying victim ... tragically final.

Bullying, which author Sheri Bauman defines as "a subset of aggression with three components: intent to harm, repetition, and a power imbalance between the bully and the target or victim," has existed since humans walked the earth. It is this unequal power, Bauman asserts, that distinguishes bullying from other forms of conflict (Bauman, 2008). With that understanding in mind, it is important to understand the way in which bullying has evolved into the global pandemic crippling so many of our youth today.

Clearly, the world has changed in innumerable ways since 1980 when *My Bodyguard* was released. Back then, we rarely heard of young people killing themselves because of bullying, and school shootings were virtually unheard of, though they did occur. Today, suicide is the second leading cause of death among young people, and suicide among ten to fourteen-year-olds has increased by more than 50% over the last thirty years. Bullying has been implicated in as much as 50% of them; moreover, 75% of school shooters have been bullied or harassed.

Bullying today is no longer confined to the "big kid picks on the smaller kid on the playground" scenario. It takes many different forms—physical, verbal, written and pictorial—and it occurs not only in the physical world of school hallways and classrooms but in the digital world via text messages, social media, and even gaming. It is everywhere, it is relentless, and for its victims, it is inescapable. One especially damaging form of bullying is relational bullying, which is more related to emotional distress caused by friends (Bauman, 2008).

Does art imitate life, or is it the other way around? In the above examples, it appears to be both. *My Bodyguard* depicts the cavalier and even comical view about bullying that was prevalent thirty-seven years ago. Essentially, that bullying is a natural part of growing up, and with the right attitude and superior muscle, it can be overcome and possibly even an enriching experience. Perhaps for a very small percentage of kids, given the times they were living in (i.e., before the dawn of the Internet and cyber-bullying) and their support systems, that was true. It was, in Clifford's case, also something one could buy their way out of. This fed into the myth that bullies are more likely to be "toughs" from lower income backgrounds. In fact, poorer kids are at a slightly greater risk of being victims. That said, bullies and victims exist across all socioeconomic groups.

13 Reasons Why also reflects truths about life for today's youth, including the increase in bullying and our evolving ideas about it. To some, however, this particular art form is not merely imitating life but influencing it. The show, which Netflix counts among its most popular, is also highly controversial—both evidenced by the fact that it was the most tweeted about show of 2017.

The show has sparked a firestorm of debate among educators, school psychologists, parents, students, and even legislators, many of whom feel it is dangerous and may inspire its teenage viewers to follow Hannah's example. For one, her suicide on the show is much more graphic than in the 2007 novel written by Jay Asher that inspired it, and two, the ability to "binge watch" all thirteen episodes means viewers can immerse themselves in Hannah's world, internalize her feelings and relate it to their own circumstances. This, along with the outcries of some prominent experts who have denounced the show as missing the mark on bullying and suicide, has prompted the National Association of School Psychologists to create guidelines to assist educators and parents when they discuss the show with students.

First and foremost, the guidelines stress that the show is not suitable for every young person. That aside, depending on how they handle it, adults can use the show to provide a safe space for kids to discuss their feelings about bullying and suicide. It can also be a tool for educators to assess individual students and see if they are being bullied and/or are at risk for engaging in self-destructive behaviors. Finally, it's an excellent way to educate parents and students about signs that someone is considering suicide, such as giving treasured items away, withdrawing from loved ones, and changes in mood.

Many people are shocked to learn that even a drastic *improvement* in one's mood (i.e., a kid who is usually depressed seems upbeat) can also be a sign that someone is suicidal. When speaking to students, it is critical to teach them never to keep another's suicidal behaviors a secret. For example, if after watching *13 Reasons Why*, a friend says they understand why Hannah did what she did, touts it as courageous, or expresses a desire to follow suit, it's time to tell an adult.

This is not just an American issue; bullying and teen suicide is a problem all over the world, and Netflix is an international streaming service. In New Zealand, a warning has been issued that kids under eighteen should not watch without an adult. While this is certainly no guarantee that young viewers won't be negatively affected, it is at least a proactive measure. All too often, steps to combat bullying are taken only after someone has ended his or her life, both in the U.S. and other countries.

In 2013, a seventeen-year-old Canadian girl named Rehtaeh Parsons attempted to hang herself after a video of her being raped was posted online. The nightmare began when the then-fifteen-year-old Rehtaeh was attacked at a party; it would continue for the next year as the video was shared and re-shared over social media. Driven to desperation and with no hope of relief, Rehtaeh decided to take her own life. Though the hanging failed, she wound up on life support and died in the hospital three days later. It was what happened next, however, that ignited outrage across the country.

After a yearlong and allegedly reluctant investigation, the attacker and the photographer were finally charged with distributing child pornography. Since the perpetrators were underage at the time, they were tried under Canada's Youth Criminal Justice Act and their identities protected. The sentence her attacker received—twelve months' probation and orders to abstain from alcohol and from contacting the victim's family (he had also reportedly threatened Rehtaeh's father)—was seen as yet another violation of Rehtaeh and a slap in the face to victims everywhere. It was only under the weight of protests and political pressure that the Canadian government enacted a law increasing the protection for cyberbullying victims and giving them the right to sue their tormentors.

This kind of tragedy is not confined to secondary education. In 2010, Rutgers University freshman Tyler Clementi killed himself after his roommate videotaped and streamed online a sexual encounter between Clementi and another male student. The eighteen-year-old Clementi had recently started coming out to his family and friends, and, after years of living under the radar in high school, he was looking forward to college life, where he believed he'd be free to live openly as a gay man. Instead, after learning via Twitter what his roommate had done (and how he was planning to do it again) he found himself the target of homophobic jokes and ridicule. A week later, he jumped off the George Washington Bridge.

After his death, the federal government enacted the Tyler Clementi High Education Anti-Harassment Act, which mandates that universities receiving federal funding must have and enforce an anti-bullying policy. Tyler's mother founded The Tyler Clementi Foundation, whose mission is to ferret out and eradicate bullying in schools, workplaces and faith-based organizations. The website provides information on the types and frequency of bullying and provides tools with which teachers, parents and students can combat bullying and prevent suicide.

Mrs. Clementi also seeks to shed light on LGBT bullying and debunk the myth that being gay and religious are not mutually exclusive and that bullying others, regardless of the reason, is the antithesis of living a faithful life. As mentioned in the chapter on the challenges facing rural America, LGBT youth in sparsely populated communities are more susceptible to being bullied and less likely to have access to support services. That said, LGBT teens and young adults are more likely to be bullied no matter where they live. According to the foundation's website, 55% of LGBT students have been cyberbullied.

Other sources report even bleaker findings. One such study included 3,767 middle-school-aged students in the southeastern and northwestern United States, with 73% of them reportedly experiencing some form of bullying, cyberbullying being the most prevalent (Rice et al., 2015). Another study focused on Lesbian, Gay, Bisexual, and Transgender (LGBT) students. 85% of the LGBT youth reported some form of bullying or harassment while at school (Swearer, Espelage, Vallancourt, & Hymel, 2010), significantly higher than the figures cited by The Tyler Clementi Foundation. Their research also found the common negative correlation between bullying victims and academic performance. They reported that the victims of bullying were less likely to be high achievers in school, while low achievement was not associated with those who bully others, (Swearer, Espelage, Vallancourt, & Hymel, 2010).

Bullying has repercussions well beyond those directly involved in it. When surveyed about their experiences with bullying, 70.6% of young people said they had witnessed bullying, as did 70.4% of school staff. It was not a rare occurrence either; in fact, 62% said they had witnessed bullying two or more times in the last month, and 41% had seen it once a week or more. Juxtaposed against these startling statistics is another from DoSomething.org: 25% of teachers still feel that bullying is not a problem, and just 4% intervene when they see it occurring.

Political writer Peggy Noonan is not surprised by the uptick in bullying or the lingering insensitivity to it; in fact, she predicted the numbers will continue to increase because, "We are the inheritors of a coarsened society.

A coarse place is by definition anti-child because it is anti-innocence."

The truth of Noonan's statement bears out in a Wall Street Journal article, "Companies Wake Up to Workplace Violence". The article highlights the dramatic increase in workplace bullying over the past two decades. In 1998, half of the workforce was reportedly bullied by colleagues and bosses. In 2017, it jumped to two-thirds. The same question applies—has bullying become a greater problem, or are we simply shining a more realistic spotlight on it?

According to Google Analytics, in 2016, there were 9.3 million visits to NoBullying.com, and DoSomething.org reports that 3.2 million American children are bullied each year. Seeing these numbers and taking into account the long-term effects of bullying, one can only imagine the damage to society.

Twenty years ago, William Copeland, a clinical psychologist at Duke University Medical Center, sought to answer this question. His study included 1,420 participants ages nine, eleven, and thirteen. Copeland reassessed each of them at age sixteen, then followed up with them again when they were nineteen, twenty-one and twenty-five.

Participants were divided into four groups: those with no involvement in bullying; those who were pure victims; those who were pure bullies; and those who had both bullied others and been bullied themselves. Copeland found that the majority—nearly 75%—were not involved with bullying. The next-largest group was the pure victims (21.6%), followed at a distance by pure bullies (5%). The smallest group was comprised of kids who had been both bullies and victims (4.5%).

The study found that pure bullies don't typically have emotional problems as adults; they used bullying to gain and maintain social status and perhaps didn't experience feelings of powerlessness as kids, at least not vis-à-vis their peers. That said, the former bullies were at higher risk for antisocial personality disorder, had less empathy for others and were less troubled by the idea of using others for their own gain. They were also more likely to abuse their spouses and kids and engage in criminal activity.

Pure victims were four times more likely than those uninvolved with bullying to experience depression, panic attacks and anxiety as adults. They were also much more likely to develop agoraphobia, which is the fear of leaving the house.

Moreover, those who experienced regular or ongoing victimization were at least twice as likely to consider ending their lives. It should be noted that other studies found that targets of serial bullying are nine times more likely to think about suicide. Female victims were more likely to attempt suicide than males.

Those who were both victims and bullies were at the greatest risk. They were five times as likely to experience depression, ten times as likely to have suicidal thoughts and fifteen times more likely to develop a panic disorder.

According to the Centers for Disease Control, twenty percent of high school students said they had been bullied, and sixteen percent said they were victims of cyberbullying. In addition, 33% of kids aged twelve to eighteen said they had been bullied once or twice a month and 27% had experienced cyberbullying once or twice a month. Bullying seemed to be more common in middle school, where 25% of bullying victims said it occurred at least once a week.

Dealing with the Bully

In the media, attention is almost exclusively focused on the victim, while the bully is seen as a nameless, faceless villain. Bullies are seen as enemy number one. However, this Davey and Goliath depiction drastically underestimates the complexity of the problem. While it is natural to rally around the victims, any real push to end bullying must also deal with the perpetrators in empowering, productive ways.

We must remember that, as reprehensible as their actions are, bullies are also children who, underneath the aggression and bravado, are hurting and often isolated. According to the American Society for the Positive Care of Children (SPCC), 30% of children admitted to bullying others in surveys. If we hope to end bullying and heal those involved, we must not ostracize or throw bullies away but teach them that they are inherently valuable human beings and can be recognized as such without having to subjugate and abuse others. To do anything less guarantees that we'll have a much larger problem down the road.

While the bulk of bullying research focuses on victims of bullying, there are studies exploring the long-term effects on the bully. Not surprisingly, the findings are both mixed and often quite grim. In addition to the issues noted above, former bullies may also have a harder time holding down a job and be more likely to engage in criminal behavior. As teenagers, a higher percentage of bullies have already been in trouble with law enforcement, and by their mid-thirties, 60% have at least one conviction. They are also more likely to carry a weapon. They seem to view the world with a "kill or be killed" mentality and believe the only way to have power is to steal it from others.

And those are just the external symptoms. Some studies have found that bullies experience higher rates of depression and anxiety. They are also more likely to develop antisocial personality disorder. This is especially true of those who realize the effects of their behavior on their victims—that's why it's so important to hold them accountable while providing emotional support and healthy coping mechanisms. Essentially, they need to recover from the bullying, or it will follow them the rest of their lives.

Like most problems that manifest at school, bullying behavior often begins at home. This is difficult for parents to hear, but the fact is that many bullies are either lacking in attention from their parents and/or siblings, or they are used to getting negative attention from them. They have likely been taught poor conflict resolution skills too, either directly or by example.

Are disagreements between the parents or among other family members settled through yelling and perhaps verbal and even physical abuse? Does someone always have to be "right," and do they achieve this by belittling another? If this behavior is part of the family dynamic, you can bet that a child will incorporate it into his/her coping mechanisms when the inevitable conflict or difficult situation arises at school.

Parents are the first line of defense in preventing their child from becoming a bully. The first step is to stop denying that the problem exists. This sounds simple, but the truth is that hearing that one's child is a bully can be just as devastating as hearing that he or she is being bullied. In fact, it can even be more so because of the component of guilt involved.

A parent who raises a bullying victim sees their child as innocent and perhaps "too nice." They can focus on comforting their son or daughter, teaching them how to stand up for themselves, and advocating on their behalf with school administrators. However, a parent who raises a bully must face the harsh truth that their parenting skills—the good, bad and the ugly—are being played out in their child's inner and outer worlds. How could they have raised such a "monster"? Parents tend to either deny the problem and/or their culpability or blame themselves for being failures.

The key here is to move past these extremes and focus on the issue at hand: how to help the child stop bullying and adopt healthy relationship skills and coping mechanisms rather than further isolating him/her and increasing his/her feelings of worthlessness.

To this end, parents should listen to both sides of the story, directly from the child(ren). Even if they believe the allegations of their child's bullying behavior to be true, it is critical for their son or daughter to feel like they have a voice. It will also give parents the opportunity to gain valuable insight into their child's world. There are several other warning signs that will help parents determine if their child is a bully. Has he/she been getting increasingly aggressive at home and/or school? Has his/her teacher called to tell the parent of disciplinary issues? Does the child tend to blame others for these and other events rather than taking responsibility for his/her actions?

If the parents conclude that their child has indeed been bullying others, they must then commit to uncovering the underlying reasons. In addition to communicating with school administrators and teachers, it may be helpful to take the child to a psychologist. A therapist's office will provide the child with a safe space in which to express their feelings without being judged as a pariah.

At the same time, bullies, regardless of their age or the reason why they engage in bullying, need to be held accountable for their behavior. This can be as simple as the behavior modification used to deal with other wrongdoings, such as taking away privileges for a certain length of time or until the child has proven themselves deserving of them. If, for example, the child has engaged in or contributed to cyberbullying, parents might take away his/her phone and restrict their Internet access to schoolwork.

Administrators are also key players in preventing and stopping bullying. Ideally, they will work with parents, but what if the alleged bully's mother and father refuse to acknowledge the problem or their role in it? Administrators must be prepared for this possibility and be willing to adhere to anti-bullying policies while demonstrating caring and concern for the welfare of all parties.

As with the parents, administrators should listen to the accounts of both the alleged bully and victim's accounts, even if they believe the allegations are true. The bully is likely feeling devalued as it is and is using bullying as a means of gaining power and acceptance from peers. That said, separate meetings should be held with each child so no intimidation can occur.

***

It is a common thing these days to go on the Internet and be faced with yet another bullying tragedy. These stories tug on our heartstrings and often result in feelings of sympathy, outrage and helplessness in the face of this seemingly insurmountable societal ill. As mentioned above, bullying takes many forms—some easily spotted, and some much more insidious, oftentimes occurring right under the noses of parents and teachers.

Relational bullying, also known as the *"Mean Girl* phenomenon" because its perpetrators and victims are mostly female, is one of the most damaging and insidious forms of bullying. It often involves the creation of cliques with strict rules for membership and harsh consequences for those who break them. If this sounds familiar, it's because, like other forms of bullying, relational bullying has been around since time began; however, it has gotten exponentially worse in the digital age.

Relational bullies use various methods of social manipulation—online and in person—to isolate and attack their victims. These include excluding them from conversations and events in and out of school, spreading rumors about the victim or telling others their secrets, and backstabbing (pretending to be her friend then "turning" on her later). "Shaming" victims for real or rumored behavior, sexual and otherwise, is also common.

Sometimes, the bullying is overt, such as openly making fun of the victim's appearance or the way she dresses or sending hurtful messages via text, email or social media, or leaving them on desks and lockers. One of the hallmarks of relational bullying is the recruitment of others through peer pressure (i.e., "Join us, or become a victim yourself.") For tweens and teens already facing immense pressures, this is exceedingly difficult to resist.

Relational bullies are largely motivated by the same reasons as any type of bully: they seek social status by eliminating competition—usually other girls they are jealous of—for popularity or the attention of boys. This is one way in which relational bullying differs from other forms of bullying—the imbalance of power is created not necessarily by the victim's inherent vulnerability; rather, the mob mentality creates that vulnerability. Relational bullies often seek to offset their own low self-esteem by targeting others. For example, a girl who does not like the way she looks will ostracize another girl, thereby drawing attention away from her own perceived shortcomings.

Relational bullies also may be seeking to create excitement in their own lives by stirring up "drama." This type of bullying is a learned behavior from television shows or even adult women they've heard gossiping. Left unchecked, it becomes part of the fabric of their socialization and a key component of the way they connect with peers, similar to an addiction.

Victims of relational bullying suffer terrible and often long-term effects. Rejection by their peers fosters and exacerbates feelings of inadequacy and depression; some even consider suicide. They are more likely to develop sleeping and eating disorders, and their academic performance often suffers. Most disturbingly, they find it difficult to form healthy friendships. The bullies are often current or former "friends," and when they go on the attack, they rob their victims of the ability to trust themselves.

Relational bullying is often difficult for adults to spot. It happens surreptitiously. When the behavior is obvious, adults often see it as the typical "cattiness" among girls and ignore it.

Cyberbullying

As seen throughout this chapter, cyberbullying has made bullying much more pervasive, insidious and dangerous. The spoken insult, though painful and damaging, is limited by time, the space in which it is said, and the audience within earshot. Those same words online are, depending on the medium, there forever and for all the world to see. Even worse, cyberbullies often employ photos and videos to further humiliate the victim. This type of bullying is usually perpetrated not by strangers on the Internet but by those in the victims' immediate social circles. Bullying campaigns begin online and then spill into school classrooms and hallways, sometimes resulting in real-life violence.

According to a study presented at the 111th Annual Meeting of American Sociological Society in 2016, a cyberbully is seven times more likely to be a friend or dating partner (current or former).

The data gathered in 2011 focused on eight hundred 8th to 12th graders attending a public school in a suburb of New York City. It found that girls were more likely to be victims of cyberbullying, and LGBTQ youths were four times more likely to be victimized than heterosexual students.

According to the Centers for Disease Control and Prevention, the suicide rate among girls ages 15 to 19 hit a forty-year high in 2015; the rate doubled from 2007 to 2015 and rose by more than 30% among boys. There is a growing body of people who believe that social media plays a significant role in this increase.

Cyberbullies are typically motivated by a desire to climb the social ladder. They usually choose victims with "juicy" secrets or because they want to get "revenge" on them for some real or perceived wrongdoing. Jealousy is another common motivator—as in the case of relational bullying, one girl might be envious of another whom boys find attractive; or a former romantic partner may be enraged when they see the Facebook posting of his ex with a new boyfriend. Thus, the campaign of hate begins.

Social media has in some ways turned us into a society of publicists, constantly spinning our own stories. As such, cyberbullies often engage in this behavior to "control the message" about a breakup. A boy who's been dumped may find it much easier to post a snarky tweet about his ex's "morals" rather than to verbally spread rumors at school. On the other hand, the threat of cyberbullying can be used to maintain control over a partner. For example, a boyfriend may threaten to post "sext messages" or revealing pictures that his soon-to-be-ex sent him.

The tactics used by cyberbullies are both varied and despicable. That said, they are hardly innovative. Like everyone else with a computer or smartphone, teens are immersed in the vitriol of Twitter wars, angry Facebook posts, and the twenty-four-hour news cycle. They are simply taking a page from the adults they see around them. It is the responsibility of the parents and administrators to understand the challenges facing youth today and to be vigilant on how online tools are being used to bully.

Most adults have heard of celebrity "roasts"—a series of people who know the roastee get up and crack jokes about his/her flaws. What people may not be aware of is that cyberbullies often use roasting to humiliate their victims, and it is anything but funny. For example, it is not unusual these days for girls who have dated the same boy to "get together" online, share his secrets and offer unflattering critiques of everything from his intelligence and sense of humor to his appearance and sexual performance.

Catfishing is a form of cyberbullying so salacious that it spawned its own documentary and television show. Catfishers create a fake online persona, which they use to "court" their victim. In the context of school bullying, the purpose is usually to elicit and expose secrets or romantic confessions. That said, there are other, far worse scenarios, in which the catfish cons money from their victims or lures them into physically dangerous "real-life" situations. Let's not forget that there is another victim here: the person(s) whose photos, names and other data have been stolen to create the false identity. It is the primary target, however, who is most at risk for humiliation, depression and even suicide.

The most famous case is the 2006 suicide of Meghan Meier, who hung herself after her "boyfriend" started calling her "fat" and other terrible names via social media. It was later revealed that he didn't even exist. More recently, Mitchell Bowie, an eighteen-year-old from the U.K., killed himself after being catfished on Facebook. His "girlfriend" had begun stalking him online and even making threatening phone calls to his house.

Another form of cyberbullying is impersonation. The bully creates a profile in the victim's name then posts rude or disturbing comments into order to get him/her in trouble.

"Slut shaming," defined as "stigmatizing a woman for engaging in behavior judged to be promiscuous or sexually provocative," has become increasingly prevalent in recent years due in large part to social media. We've all seen it, usually in the form of a Twitter war about and between celebrities, but all too often this particularly cruel form of cyberbullying hits much closer to home and is leveled against girls unable to handle it.

The perpetrator will share some explicit or otherwise compromising photo of the victim along with some caption criticizing her clothing or behavior. The goal here is to "expose" her as someone with "loose morals." Slut-shaming is a favorite for ex-romantic partners seeking to humiliate someone who broke off with them, and, to this end, they also share private text messages. That said, the most vicious slut-shaming is often perpetrated by females, so much so that in 2016 Teen Vogue published an article entitled, "6 Ways You May Be Slut-Shaming Without Realizing It." In it, Emily Linden, author and creator of *The UnSlut Project*, counsels young women on bullying and how they can recognize, take responsibility for their own slut-shaming and hopefully stop contributing to a toxic culture.

This includes things like blaming a girl when a nude photo of her is stolen and posted online; revealing information about someone's sexual behavior (i.e., a friend confides in you that she slept with a guy on the first date); or publicly holding girls to a sexual double standard (i.e., jumping on the bandwagon when a guy posts something lewd about her).

Bottom line: Linden is advocating for girls to stand up for each other, as this would go a long way toward taking the sting and eventually the steam out of slut-shaming. It would be as simple as a group of girls stepping in to defend someone who was shamed by her ex.

"Subtweeting" and "Vaguebooking" involve insulting and tormenting the victim without actually using their name. Enough is said, however, that everyone, including the target, knows who's being spoken about. Like other forms of cyberbullying, it contributes to a climate of fear for everyone; it is also difficult for adults to prove.

Public shaming is yet another form of cyberbullying. Think of it as a digital Salem Witch Trial. One's "wrong-doing"—real or perceived—is posted online for all the world to see. Others jump on the bandwagon to attack the victim. These "secondary bullies" feel justified in doing so because they believe the victim deserves it.

Combatting cyberbullying can sometimes be an uphill battle. In order to fight it, adults must first be aware that it is going on and take it seriously. Adults also must understand that, for better or worse, social media is not some fad but a part of our kids' lives for the foreseeable future.

In November of 2017, Ashawnty Davis, a ten-year-old from Aurora, Colorado, committed suicide after a fight between her and another student was videotaped and posted on the site Musical.ly. The other student had allegedly been bullying Ashawnty, which was the reason for the confrontation, and, according to her parents, the bullying afterward at the hands of her fellow fifth graders drove her to take her own life. The parents blamed the school for not intervening; specifically, they claimed the school had denied their request to meet with the parents of the other kids involved. Had administrators facilitated such a meeting, Davis' parents said, their daughter might still be alive.

The school's representative, after stating that they have a zero-tolerance policy on bullying, claimed they were never made aware of Ashawnty's predicament. Furthermore, she pointed out that the fight, which had occurred on school grounds, happened after school hours. This leaves several unanswered questions, namely, why was the bullying before the fight never noticed by administrators? Did it occur online or in real life? Were her parents aware of it? And possibly the biggest questions of all: why were fifth graders on school grounds, presumably unsupervised, after school hours, and does this exonerate the school from responsibility? The answers, elusive as they may be, all add up to one thing: we need to do better if we're going to protect other kids like Ashawnty.

In the wake of such a tragedy, many asked themselves how someone so young could be so desperate that they believe ending their life is the only way out. Perhaps they even thought that Ashawnty Davis was a rare case, that something must be "wrong" with her. This attitude is indicative of a fundamental misunderstanding of the world in which today's kids live. They don't fondly recall the days before text messages or Twitter or Facebook; in fact, they don't remember those days at all. Social media has always been their reality; however, that doesn't mean they know how to handle the pressures of it. As those charged with their care, adults must stop burying their heads in the sand and learn to assimilate with that lifestyle and integrate it with proper advice and counseling.

Take, for example, Yik Yak, the once popular, now defunct chat app. Created in 2013, by two college students, the app distinguished itself by making all users anonymous.

First seen as a bastion of free speech, complaints about racist and misogynist language soon started flooding in. However, an MIT study comparing it to Twitter found that anonymity was not necessarily Yik Yak's problem. Users were instead put off by another unique feature: Yik Yak was extremely localized (users had to be within ten miles of each other). When someone is making fun of your appearance, intelligence, et cetera, they are literally around the corner ... or across the classroom. This would be painful for people of any age, so one could only imagine how terrible it was for children to live in this fishbowl.

Whatever form bullying takes, the fear of harassment is real, and it is daily, making one question the accuracy of even the worst statistics, as victims may fear reprisal. Even the fear of lawsuits has not curbed the issue, as schools have not typically been held liable for bullying incidences so long as they have made some reasonable effort to intervene (Wood, 2012). This is even after Davis v. Monroe County Board of Education (1999), which held that private action damages could be filed against a federal-funded school board when it acts with deliberate indifference to acts of student-on-student harassment.

This case initiated the five-part harassment test to determine public school liability. However, the test only includes the following components for "protected" students: the student belongs to a statutorily protected category (race/ethnicity, gender, sexual preference, disability, etc.), the student was harassed because of this protected trait, the harassment was so severe that the student was deprived of access to educational benefits, school officials knew of the harassment, and school officials were deliberately indifferent to the harassment.

In L.W. v. Toms River Board of Education, a New Jersey court found the school liable for sexual orientation peer harassment. The district had a zero-tolerance discrimination policy but did not reinforce it. From this case, it was noted that school districts are only shielded from liability when their actions (preventative and remedial) are reasonable in the light of the totality of the circumstances (McArdle, 2013).

In Georgia, the DeKalb County School District entered into a landmark settlement agreement with the U.S. Department of Justice after they got involved in a bullying matter with a Sikh student. Caught up in the September 11th backlash, this middle school student had been bullied for years based on his religion and national origin. This case had Title IX implications, and the agreement required the district to provide trainings for students and staff on religious and national origin harassment (The SIKH Coalition, 2013).

While the above cases are certainly a step in the right direction (not to mention politically expedient), they beg the question: aren't we supposed to be protecting *all* students? What about the obese child? How about the child with facial scars? What happens when a student is bullied because they are simply small in stature? Or because their grades are too low or too high? This is very common in today's schools, and we, as a society, still do not know how to address it, much less stop it.

Those administrators who do try to fight cyberbullying often find that their hands are tied by First Amendment concerns. They are afraid of losing a lawsuit or even their jobs, which, to be honest, is a possibility when a bully asserts his/her right to free speech. However, this right does have exceptions (i.e., hate speech or speech that mentions a person's race or disability, et cetera,) and it is the responsibility of every administrator to understand them so that we can act not out of fear but in the best interest of the children whose care we are charged with.

For example, in Kowalski v. Berkeley County Schools, a student sued the school district after being disciplined for creating "Students Against Sluts Herpes," a website that named individual students. The ensuing bullying of these students became so severe that one stopped coming to school. The creator of the site was then given a five-day suspension and kicked off the cheerleading squad. She argued that the school could not sanction off-campus speech, but the courts disagreed because the speech created substantial disorder and disruption at school and therefore was not protected under the First Amendment (Whitted + Takiff Law, 2016).

Hate speech is easy enough to spot, but what happens when a student speaks in general terms or subliminally mentions something meant to solicit a response? Cyberbullying is evolving as quickly as technology itself, and administrators not up on the latest website or app don't even know it is happening. It is also difficult to discern administrators' roles in investigating cyberbullying situations, mainly because it can occur while participants are at home, in a public place or some other area outside school property.

But what happens when the children come to school? It

is no longer cyber. It is now a face-to-face encounter with those who were part of the incidences, and that world comes crashing in around them because they can't just turn off their device.

Eight-year-old Gabriel Taye committed suicide a few days after a mysterious incident occurred in the bathroom of his Cincinnati elementary school. The security tape shows Gabriel interacting with another child then falling on the floor. Other children stepped over his body for several minutes and even poked him. A police officer who reviewed the security tape said it was bullying and possibly an assault but felt it should be handled at the school level because the children involved were so young.

Phillip Lee (2016) urges schools to adopt a "nexus" and "foreseeability" test, which combines approaches used by federal courts when analyzing the constitutionality of the disciplinary actions of school officials in situations where the bullying took place off-site (e.g., social media). Lee stresses that these approaches effectively balance the competing interests of protecting cyberbullying victims and protecting students' free speech rights, (Lee, 2016 p. 888-889).

What Lee is not considering is that schools' ability to gain the knowledge of these acts is directly tied to trust, cooperation, and relationships with students, parents, teachers and the communities as a whole. Cyberbullying, or any act of bullying, is many times not public and not exposed without a freeway of information that flows both ways. In other words, today's children are experiencing fear not just from actions originating and occurring within the school boundaries but in a virtual world in which they are under the belief that only they truly understand.

Kub and Feldman (2015) offer suggestions on how these collaborations can occur. They suggest that districts build healthy public policy by consulting school psychologists and nurses when creating anti-bullying policies. Districts should create supportive environments in which collaboration between the different groups works to promote the safety of children in the school environment. Community actions should be strengthened in order to gain support and raise awareness of the anti-bullying efforts. Personal skills should be developed through school-wide prevention activities and health services reoriented to provide a fuller, more accurate picture of the child. Brewer (2017) addresses the whole child model, which calls for school districts to focus, not just on academic success but social and emotional health as well. This may help minimize factors that contribute to bullying.

Parents also play a critical role in putting an end to cyberbullying. First, they must be aware of the sites their kids visit—they can do this by using parental controls and "friending" their kids on social media. They should also advise their kids against giving their passwords to anyone, including friends, or opening unidentifiable messages. Most importantly, they must teach their children that when they post something online, it is potentially accessible by anyone. This includes pictures, so they should know not to post anything they would not want their parents and grandparents to see. Promoting prudent posting habits will also save them trouble down the road when potential employers look at their digital footprint.

Administrators and parents can combat bullying by encouraging kids to extend kindness to bullying victims. Whether the bullying is in person or on social media, the bullies' powers lie in numbers. If others refuse to follow them, that power quickly deflates. Children should understand that when they befriend a bullying victim (i.e., include them in social activities and so on) they might even be saving a life.

CHAPTER 2
One Size Does Not Fit All

"At the end of the day, you can either focus on what's tearing you apart or what's holding you together."

—*Unknown*

Johnathon is an eighth grader from the Mott Haven section of the Bronx. Though it is only roughly eleven acres in size, Mott Haven is overcrowded with a population of approximately 53,000 people. It is also one of the poorest neighborhoods in New York City and has high crime rates—both to person and property—relative to the rest of the city.

Johnathon lives in a small two-bedroom apartment with his mother and two younger siblings. His mother is an office worker earning minimum wage, and though living quarters are extremely tight, they cannot afford to move. In the meantime, they have applied for the housing lottery, a citywide program that helps connect low-income families with affordable housing.

There are several schools—some good, some bad—within walking distance from their home, so Johnathon is able to drop his siblings off at their highly rated charter elementary school before continuing on to his own school. Johnathon's mother cannot afford to get him a computer, but thanks to a donation to his school from a wealthy local philanthropist, he has a loaner laptop to do research, complete his homework and upload it to his teacher. His mother worries for his safety in the rough neighborhood but hopes that the after-school anti-violence programs available will help him stay the course, stay off drugs and one day go to college.

Billy, who is also an eighth grader, hails from Golconda, a tiny, picturesque town in Pope County, Illinois. The county, though large geographically (374 square miles), is sparsely populated with just under 12,000 residents. It has been struggling with poverty for half a century, a problem exacerbated by the closure of coal mines in the 1980s. Since then, the picture has become even bleaker with a declining population, a scarcity of jobs, and multigenerational poverty. The schools were also dramatically affected, with many falling into such disrepair that the state board of education took them over in 2001. In 2013, the county regained control, but many of the problems, including that of acquiring qualified teachers, remain.

Billy comes from a long line of coal miners, but these days, it is difficult for his father to find work. Billy's mother works at a local grocery store and earns only about $14,000 a year. They've nearly lost their home several times and often struggle just to put food on the table.

Billy's bus ride to middle school is over an hour each way, meaning he has to get up at five a.m. He arrives already tired and sometimes hungry as well, either because he didn't have time to eat or because there wasn't much food at home. Once there, he shares textbooks with another student; his whole class shares one computer. Internet access is intermittent at best, so his teacher has given up on using YouTube and other online tools to teach them. Like many of his classmates, Billy does not have his own computer, and even if he did, the Internet at his house is no faster than dial-up, making uploading his homework impossible.

Bored, fatigued and anxious about the problems at home, Billy soon starts to see school as a waste of time. What is the point of studying American history or reading novels when his parents can barely make ends meet? In a few years, he will be thinking about quitting altogether so he can find factory work and help support the family.

Neither of the above scenarios is ideal. In fact, they are both shameful and all-too-common examples of the hardships facing poor children in the U.S. Yet, they also highlight some of the unique challenges facing students in rural areas.

It is impossible to understand the challenges facing rural schools without first addressing the larger issues of rural America. Ask anyone who lives there, and they will tell of you the many benefits to rural living, including fresh air, wide open spaces and a connection to nature. Rural towns, which are defined as those having less than 2,500 residents, are often lovelier, cleaner and safer than suburban and urban areas. Homes are also much more affordable, and there is a strong sense of community. If given the choice, most people from rural areas would prefer to live and work in the towns they grew up in.

On the other hand, this vast area often touted as "the heartland" has been marginalized politically, financially, and educationally. This bears out in recent statistics, which show the revitalization of previously depressed and dangerous areas of New York and Philadelphia and a slow but dramatic decline of rural communities. Industries that used to support these regions have faltered—whether due to a lack of resources, as in the case of timber, or because of industrialization, as in the case of coal mining.

Either scenario has led to a loss of jobs, business closures and widespread poverty and population decline (while 72% of the country's geography is "nonmetropolitan," only 15% of the population lives in these areas, and that number is falling). These changes have even affected the agricultural industry, with mom-and-pop farms being swallowed by larger corporate concerns. Many of America's most beautiful small towns are mere shells of their former glory, and their residents are fighting an uphill battle to survive. The extent of their despair bears out in the current suicide statistics. In the past sixteen years, the suicide rate in the country has increased by 40%. In rural America, that portion is 40% higher than the national average and 83% higher than in urban areas.

Nowhere is this tragic story more apparent than in the education system. Nearly half the school boards in the U.S. are in rural areas—this means nine million of fifty million public school children—yet they are woefully neglected by everyone from journalists to politicians.

There is even a lack of adequate research on these areas, making it difficult to understand the complexity of the issues let alone construct creative solutions. For those who live and work in these areas, however, the crisis is all too real.

Even national education experts often miss the mark. When asked what the biggest challenge facing rural areas is, they usually cite the lack of teachers and technology. While these are certainly important issues, rural administrators cited too little money for special education mandates, too much paperwork, and too many strings attached to funding. The money is often earmarked for one thing when the school is in desperate need of a structural improvement. In other words, the bureaucratic model used in cities is oftentimes not a good fit for rural areas.

In urban areas, poverty is easy to spot. One walks by dilapidated buildings and homeless people; law enforcement officers maintain a noticeable presence to keep the peace, and there is probably a plethora of billboards advertising services for vulnerable populations. This is a sharp contrast to rural towns, where one can drive by modest but livable homes nestled in picturesque hills or cornfields with no clue that the people inside are struggling to buy clothes for their kids and keep the electric on. The fact is, rural areas have higher rates of poverty, unemployment and malnutrition, and since school districts cover large geographical areas, educators are often unaware of how their students are living. This becomes apparent later in the form of poor educational outcomes and increased crime, drug abuse and dropout rates.

The faltering economy coupled with fewer cultural attractions and services and the lingering bias about rural people has made it exceedingly difficult to attract talented teachers, especially since the salaries are rarely if ever competitive with urban school districts.

In McDowell County, where Billy in the above hypothetical lives, there is a constant struggle to hire and retain teachers. Between 2013 and 2016, the school system hired 137 teachers, but 163 quit. Substitute teachers, usually those with no training in the particular subject, were brought in to fill the gap. It is a familiar story all across rural Americas, including the Midwest, the South, and the Northeast.

As a result, rural students are less likely to go to college. Their high school experience has left them ill-prepared, particularly in math and science. In addition, unlike their urban counterparts, students in rural areas don't see different avenues to and examples of success, which leads to the sentiment that higher education is a waste of time. Rural students are also more likely to want to remain close to home, not only because they enjoy rural living but to help their families financially.

Even getting to and from school poses different and often more significant challenges for rural students. There is a wide variance depending upon where one lives, but for many children, large geographical areas and fewer schools equal lengthy commutes. They have to get up hours before classes start and then sit on the bus for an hour or more. They often arrive at school already tired and then have to do the whole thing all over again at the end of the day. It is no surprise, then, that lengthy commutes have been linked to lower educational outcomes. It might also make participating in after-school activities difficult, either because kids have to get home for dinner or simply because the buses aren't running by the time the activity ends.

Long bus rides are also expensive, as the school must pay for the fuel and the driver's time. The obvious answer is to build more schools, but over the past several years, population decline has led to more and more school closures. Post-industrialization and mine closures have left thousands out of work. Families go in search of jobs, leaving more defunct business in their wake. Each time a school loses a student, it also loses thousands in funding, thus perpetuating the vicious cycle.

The Digital Divide

Think of everything you do in a day that requires the Internet. You send and receive emails, pay your bills, search for information and directions. The list goes on and on. Think of how frustrated you get when your Internet goes down or runs a bit slow. Your productivity is decreased or nonexistent, costing you time and perhaps even money. Now imagine what your life would be like if you did not have access to the Internet; you'd feel like you were back in the Stone Age. Well, believe it or not, millions of Americans face this every day. For people living in cities and suburban areas, it is difficult to fathom the far-reaching ramifications in nearly every area of life.

The FCC defines "fast" internet at a minimum download speed of 25 Mbps (megabits per second)—somewhere between the 100 Mbps common in most cities and old-fashioned dial-up, which downloaded at a rate of less than 1 Mbps. The FCC estimates that 39% of rural residents—roughly twenty-three million people—do not have access to fast service, compared with only four percent of urbanites. Many people have to drive miles from their home to access the Internet, which severely handicaps their ability to live and work in the modern world.

A lack of Internet access makes it difficult for rural residents to utilize online banking and insurance tools. It also puts farmers at a disadvantage, who are unable to digitally monitor crops and ranchers who cannot buy and sell cattle online. Forcing them to rely on "old-fashioned" forms of transactions severely handicaps their viability in the marketplace. For a town, a lack of connectivity plays into every rural stereotype and adds to the difficulty in attracting new businesses and residents.

In some areas, 911 call centers regularly lose their Internet connection, meaning they cannot look up arrest records or license plates. Local authorities cannot track weather patterns and fast-moving, potentially dangerous storm centers. And, in a world where our healthcare system increasingly relies on the Internet, doctors in rural areas cannot view scans and blood work results or send them to colleagues for consultation.

Expense and geography remain the largest barriers to making modern Internet available. Most rural areas are still using existing telephone technology and copper lines to get online rather than the fiber optic cable needed for high-speed broadband. The estimated cost to install fiber optics is around $30,000 per mile, which, given the vast geographical regions in the Midwest and South, adds up to billions of dollars. There are not enough customers to offset that price tag, so it is not uncommon for people to get monthly quotes of hundreds of dollars for relatively slow connections.

For those who think cellular data can pick up the slack, think again. First, there is often a monthly cap on such data, and overages lead to exorbitant charges. Also, satellite dishes, which are often used in conjunction with wireless networks, are not as fast as broadband and insufficient to run a business, healthcare facility or school.

Like so many other challenges facing rural America, the Digital Divide has only recently garnered any serious attention from the national media. It rarely even came up in the many conversations about income discrepancy, though it is certainly a contributing factor. That said, it has been on the radar of companies, philanthropic concerns and governmental agencies for some time. Microsoft's Rural Airband Initiative would, in partnership with Internet providers, use television "white space" to send Internet data over unused broadcast frequencies. The ten-billion-dollar initiative plans to bring Internet to two million people by 2022, which is certainly admirable but will barely make a dent in the overwhelming need.

Nowhere is this need more urgent than in the school system. A lack of Internet severely hampers teachers' efforts to create a level playing field and makes superior education impossible. They cannot access tools like YouTube EDU, a vast library containing more than 700,000 videos, as well as Moodle and other learning management systems that facilitate online collaboration; virtual classes; and peer assessment of assignments. Oftentimes, students are not even able to digitally submit their homework and papers, which leads to delays and/or the added expense of having to print out their work. There is also less access to e-books and Google Docs.

Essentially, children in these areas are confined to another age. They grow up less proficient in technology and are at a disadvantage when and if they do go to college, get jobs, or run their own businesses. This point leads to another myth about rural areas: everyone works for someone else—usually a factory or coal mine. The truth is, rural residents have a strong entrepreneurial spirit rivaling those of any big city.

By necessity, this includes teachers and administrators. Inadequate staffing means that they must often wear many hats—i.e., the school principal may also teach math classes and drive the bus. There is no such thing as "not my job"; everyone must be willing to pitch in and help. By the same token, bureaucratic structures that work in urban schools are often not a good fit in rural areas, where teachers must be able to come up with creative, out-of-the-box solutions free of earmarks and other financial constraints.

Oftentimes, however, the educational establishment does not understand rural needs. They read the same sparse research and, since they rarely travel to rural areas, are subject to many of the same myths as the public.

When they do try to address the problem, it is with the same solutions applied—often with great success—to urban schools. However, these are often not viable options for rural and remote areas.

Let's return for a moment to the hypothetical at the beginning of the chapter. Clearly, Johnathon faces significant socioeconomic challenges that threaten not only his ability to realize academic benchmarks and eventually find gainful employment but to stay safe in an environment where gangs and drugs are a constant presence. Gangs in particular can be tempting; they offer vulnerable youth the protection found in numbers as well as ways to make money. Even with the persistent, combined effort of his mother, teachers, and law enforcement, Johnathon and his siblings are at risk of falling prey to them every time he leaves the apartment.

That said, there are still very real differences between Johnathon's challenges and those facing his counterpart, Billy. For one, there are organizations offering activities to urban at-risk youths to keep them away from criminal elements and drugs, and programs that donate computers to the school and even extras for kids to bring home.

While he lives in a cramped apartment now, his family has a chance to move to a bigger place in the future; it is also possible that the revitalization efforts currently germinating in the South Bronx will eventually impact his neighborhood. High-speed broadband is available at his home and school, which means Johnathon can upload his homework, and his teacher is able to incorporate a combination of digital and organic tools into the curriculum. Most importantly, Johnathon can keep abreast of ever-changing technology.

For Billy, however, the lack of such a network makes overcoming such challenges exponentially harder. In the past year, three factories have closed in his area, creating a domino effect. Hundreds lost their jobs, and without their patronage, other businesses—most of them mom-and-pops—also went under. Many families have since left town in search of other opportunities, including two teachers whose spouses could not find work.

Enrollment at Billy's school has also declined, and with it, funding for everything from administrators' salaries to structural repairs. As a result, the school has been unable to replace its foreign language teacher, and several classrooms have leaky roofs. There is no art or music program and no after-school activities.

Residents who have stayed are facing chronic unemployment, but except for churches and a Salvation Army store, there are no non-profit organizations to help low-income families. Crimes to persons and property are also on the rise thanks to the growing opioid problem in the area. Many of the townspeople are addicted to some kind of painkiller, and all of them will do anything to finance their habit.

As the above demonstrates, measures taken in cities are often not feasible in rural and remote areas. One of the most glaring examples of this is school choice, which has been touted in urban and suburban areas. In sparsely populated regions, the "good" school might be one hundred or more miles away, making it impossible for kids to get to. The same is true for charter schools, which have been responsible for dramatic educational improvements in cities like New York but tend to be viewed with a wary eye by rural residents, and for good reason. Perhaps this is why, to date, of the seven thousand charters in the U.S., only one thousand are located in rural areas.

As noted above, rural public schools are chronically underfunded, both with regard to their own needs and relative to those in suburban and urban areas. This is due in large part to sparse populations and smaller tax bases. In addition, federal and state mandates minimize other badly needed resources (e.g., for special education). Charters and other nontraditional schools draw more students and precious funding dollars away from institutions that are already strapped for cash.

In addition, private, parochial, and nontraditional schools can pick and choose students per their particular mission and guidelines, whether that means kids who excel in STEM or those with perfect behavioral histories. It stands to reason, therefore, that evidence of these schools' successes is skewed. Public schools, on the other hand, are legally bound to take everyone, regardless of his or her socioeconomic status and learning and/or mental health challenges. These challenges then affect test scores, crime and bullying, and substance abuse statistics to name a few.

I am not contending that in and of themselves these efforts cannot be successful. For example, Kipp Delta Schools, a network of charters in Arkansas, has grown from one middle school with sixty-five students in 2002 to six campuses serving more than 1,400 students, most of whom come from low-income families, and the schools continue to defy regional expectations. Of the class of 2017, 95% graduated, 81% went on to college, and 47% went on to get a four-year degree, surpassing both U.S. (81%, 64%, and 45% respectively) and low-income (47%, 34%, and 9% respectively) averages. One of Kipp's schools has even been ranked the fourth-best high school in the state. Clearly, they are doing something right, and perhaps their model is worth studying for purposes of improving the public school system.

That said, even this success story highlights rural challenges. Kipp has thirty buses that travel a collective thousand miles a day to bring students to and from school—an enormous expenditure of time and money. Like other rural schools, it also faces the constant challenge of attracting and retaining skilled teachers, whether because potential candidates are dissuaded by the lack of amenities in the area or the lack of other industries makes it difficult for their spouses to find work. While in a vacuum, Kipp's schools are an example of what can be achieved; it only emphasizes the need for more funding of our public schools.

Free public education is one of our society's most treasured values, and it is incumbent upon parents, legislators and other stakeholders to honor that value by properly supporting public institutions rather than abandoning them for the next shiny new thing.

In the absence of adequate state and federal funding, philanthropic efforts around education have been a cause for hope. Historically, most philanthropists have focused on urban areas. There are, however, organizations making significant contributions in rural school districts. For example, The Niswonger Foundation has partnered with the Care Foundation of America to prepare students in Northern Tennessee for college. The initiative (NiswongerCARE College Access Reaches Everyone) has impacted approximately 30,000 high school students.

Other philanthropies take creative approaches targeted to rural needs. I support these efforts to the extent that they seek to partner with public schools. The Wisconsin-based Kern Family Foundation has focused its philanthropic efforts on STEM subjects (science, technology, engineering and math), areas in which rural school districts often suffer the greatest teacher deficit.

Kern-funded programs also cultivate "an entrepreneurial mindset," which is defined as fostering curiosity and creativity so that students can be competitive in the marketplace, whether they have their own businesses or work for someone else. It also emphasizes students' ability not only to celebrate their achievements but to learn and move on from failures, a factor identified by thought leaders and titans of industry alike as a key component of personal and professional success. Perhaps most importantly, the foundation also subsidizes Teach for America's "Rural School Leadership Academy," which trains teachers to be administrators with an understanding of rural needs.

Still, others present a great cause of concern for the future of public education in rural areas. For example, the goal of the Donnell-Kay Foundation's "ReSchool" initiative is for 50,000 students to be in "unconventional school forms" by 2030. These school forms include new ways of measuring success rather than relying on standardized testing. While I certainly agree that these tests are being given far too much weight, I have to ask, first, how this foundation will choose the 50,000 students it accepts, and how the loss of those students will affect funding for the public schools servicing their areas.

Similarly, the Albertson Foundation, which over the last fifty years has funded education in Idaho to the tune of more than $650 million, focuses on social entrepreneurship and nontraditional schools. One of its more recent initiatives is Bluum, a "new school incubator."

While the motives of these organizations should be applauded and perhaps even be part of educational goal-setting moving forward, their implementation will likely have unfortunate consequences on public schools that administrators cannot afford to ignore.

Some organizations such as Kahn Academy have recognized these concerns. Kahn, which was created in 2012 as a pilot program to determine whether online learning helps rural students, originally operated outside the educational system. Since then, however, it has begun partnering with school districts to bring personalized learning to the classroom. At the time of this writing, the program has grown to reach 10,000 students in over thirty-three districts. It also pays for necessary research on rural education.

Clearly, public schools in rural America need more funding. There also needs to be fewer strings attached to that funding so that stakeholders with expertise on the particular and multifaceted needs of rural America can put it to the best use. This is an old argument, and any ground gained can just as quickly be lost with the arrival of a new administration, the adoption of a new bill, changes in the tax laws, and so on. Yet, even in the face of these seemingly insurmountable obstacles, strides are being made at the local level.

Many rural schools share teachers, who either travel between locations or, when possible, deliver their lessons using video technology. Other schools have come together to form sports teams, art programs, and other invaluable extracurricular activities. These grassroots efforts have enriched the lives of thousands of rural students and are the greatest source of hope until more wide-sweeping changes can be implemented.

The Opioid Epidemic

It used to be that drugs were the scourge of the inner city. Anyone around in the 1980s has heard of the "Cocaine Cowboys" in Miami and the crack epidemic in Harlem, with countless people incarcerated, homeless or dead. Back then, no one could have anticipated that drugs would similarly ravage America's heartland or that its genesis would lie not with dealers on the street but in doctors' offices. The substance problem is certainly not limited to opioids, however. Alcohol abuse continues to be a problem among rural youth, and according to the Center on Addiction and Substance Abuse, eighth graders in rural and remote areas are 83% more likely to smoke crack, and 30% of people said heroin was "easy to get" in their town. Other data shows a greater increase in rural areas of babies born addicted to opioids.

In 2015, overdose death rates in rural areas surpassed those of cities. Moreover, rural residents were four times more likely to die of an overdose in 2015 than in 1999. The states hit hardest by addiction include New Hampshire, West Virginia and Kentucky.

Most addicts can trace their drug use to a physical injury, usually one that took place while working on a farm or in a factory. Rural areas typically lack alternative healthcare services like physical therapy, forcing doctors to rely on painkillers such as oxycodone, Percocet, and Vicodin. Patients have two choices—take the meds or deal with chronic pain that robs them of their quality of life and the ability to work. With mouths to feed and few employment options, this amounts to no choice at all. Before they know it, they require more and more pills to get them through the day. When their doctor catches on, they buy them on the street. When the habit becomes too expensive, they often turn to a cheaper high—heroin.

Injuries are not the only reason for the escalation of drug use. Rural areas have not recovered from the Great Recession like the rest of the country, resulting in chronic financial stress. That, coupled with social isolation, a higher rate of abuse found in rural areas, and a pervasive feeling of hopelessness, has created a breeding ground for widespread drug abuse. It is also easier to get drugs in these small towns. It may seem counterintuitive, but rural residents interact with twice as many people as those in cities; these wider social circles have created more opportunities to buy drugs. The close communities that are so much a fabric of rural life become a double-edged sword—drug users have a particularly strong bond and are willing to keep each other's secrets.

Those who want to get help with their addiction find that treatment centers are few and far between. The nearest one may be a hundred miles away, and for someone with no car or time to get there, it might as well be a thousand. Trying to get clean on their own, especially from heroin, is all but impossible. Suboxone, an opioid that weans people off heroin without the side effects, can only be prescribed by doctors with a special license, and these doctors are very scarce.

These factors, along with the stigma attached to addiction, have led some people to suffer in silence rather than seek treatment. For many, the pain of telling the doctor they've seen since childhood is worse than the problem itself. The biggest victims, however, are once again rural children who are either living with addicted parents or enticed to use drugs to escape their harsh realities. As with so many rural challenges, outside-the-box thinking is needed if this epidemic is to be addressed.

One promising option is telemedicine, through which patients interact with doctors via phone or Skype. While, generally, telemedicine has been on the rise in recent years, it is now being strongly considered for those attempting to kick their drug habit. Each state has its own laws, but for the most part patients still have to travel to a participating healthcare provider, who then establishes an online connection with the therapist or doctor prescribing the Suboxone or methadone.

Violence

As mentioned earlier, one of the primary benefits of rural life is that it is safer than living in the city. While this may be true overall, it has certainly not been the case for children. In fact, bullying is even more prevalent in America's smallest towns. Other chapters will address bullying and other forms of school violence in greater detail. This section focuses on specific challenges facing rural students as compared to their suburban and urban counterparts.

According to a 2015 report by Indicators of Crime and School Safety, there were fifty-three victimizations per one-thousand students in rural areas. This was almost double the rate of suburbia, with twenty-eight victimizations per thousand students and much higher than cities, with thirty-two victimizations per thousand students. Many of these incidents take place on the bus to and from school, and, as mentioned earlier, rural students have much longer commutes, meaning they are stuck in a confined space with their torturers for significant chunks of time each day.

In recent years, much attention has been given to the bullying of students due to their sexual orientation. In every area of the country, students who identify as lesbian, gay, bisexual or transgender (LGBT) face greater challenges around acceptance and are prone to higher rates of school violence and even suicide. These challenges are even greater in rural areas.

A 2016 report from the Gay, Lesbian and Straight Education Network (GLSEN) highlighted the challenges facing rural LGBT youth. Typically, these students experienced a lack of inclusive curricula and an awareness on the part of educators. Oftentimes, neither sexual orientation or gender identity was mentioned in the school's anti-violence policy, and indeed, a feeling of being unsafe (whether real or perceived) led to lower GPAs, more truancy and decreased goal-setting and ambitions for life post-high school, including plans to attend college. In fact, 36% of LGBT students reported missing at least one class or school day because they didn't feel safe, higher than the 30% of suburban and urban students who said the same.

This problem is exacerbated by a lack of services such as support groups and Gay-Straight Alliances that have been so helpful in other areas. Just 27% of rural LGBT students reported having GSAs at their school, whereas 55% of suburban and 53% of urban kids reported the same. When GSAs were present, however, rural students were more likely to take advantage of these groups. In addition, schools with other support networks had LGBT populations that were, as a whole, more connected and reported fewer instances of victimization.

In the past year, the vast majority (87%) of rural LGBT students reported being verbally harassed for their sexual orientation, with 91% reporting that they had heard the word "gay" used in a pejorative way (i.e., calling a straight student gay as a means of insulting him/her). The harassment was not limited to words either. Another 45% of LGBT students were physically harassed (i.e., pushed or shoved), and 22% reported an actual assault. They often stated that they felt particularly unsafe in locker rooms, bathrooms, and gym class.

Non-conforming gender expression (i.e., clothes and hairstyles) also attracted the attention of bullies, with 68% of rural LGBT students reporting verbal harassment, 31% reporting physical harassment, and 16% reporting physical assault at school over the past year. Many students regularly heard remarks about boys and girls who behaved in non-conforming ways (e.g., boys who were not "masculine enough" and girls who were not "feminine enough").

Adding to their distress was a lack of responsiveness from administrators and other school staff. When asked whether personnel came to their defense, just 13% of LGBT students said that staff intervened "always or most of the time" when they heard homophobic remarks. An even smaller portion, 11%, reported that staff intervened upon hearing remarks about gender expression. It is important to note that such bullying tactics are often leveled at heterosexual students who are "accused" of being gay, both at school and through social media. Oftentimes, the victims are gender non-conforming; other times, the bullies simply choose what they believe will cause their victims the most distress. These students experience the same fear, isolation, and depression, with none of the support services (as scarce as they may be) available to those in the LGBT community.

This was part of a less accepting culture overall with regard to LGBT issues. While 18% and 20% of suburban and urban students, respectively, reported learning positive things about LGBT-related events in history, just 11% of rural LGBT students reported having such an inclusive curriculum.

And of those whose schools did have internet access, a smaller portion (39%) of rural LGBT students were able to get on LGBT websites, compared to 44% of suburban students and 44% of urban students. Smaller percentages of rural LGBT students also reported having supportive administrators and fellow students than their suburban and urban counterparts.

Finally, rural children are at much higher risk of committing suicide. A 2015 study published by JAMA Pediatrics examined suicide rates among ten to twenty-four-year-olds from 1996 and 2010 and found that the rate for rural youth was double that of urban areas. While that gap has always existed, the study also showed that it has only widened over time. While many of those suicides were committed with guns, this may simply be because rural youth have more access to firearms. In fact, all methods of suicide, including hangings and overdoses, had increased.

CHAPTER 3
Normalizing the Abnormal

"We live in a society that believes it can define normal and then judge everything against that fictitious standard."

—*Margaret Wheatley*

In the mid-1990s, psychologist Gretchen LeFever Watson noticed an exceptionally high number of children being diagnosed and medicated for ADHD in her community in southeastern Virginia. With funding by the Centers for Disease Control (CDC), LeFever Watson spearheaded an effort to research the issue, learn the reasons behind the diagnoses, and hopefully improve care for children with behavioral issues.

Throughout her work, she found herself continually maligned by colleagues who were in collusion with pharmaceutical companies. They accused her of falsely reporting the high rates of diagnosis and prescribing of meds; one person even submitted an anonymous letter to her medical school accusing her of academic fraud. In 2005, Watson's computers were confiscated, her research buried, and the project shut down. This was despite the fact that she had amassed a wealth of information about over-diagnosing and prescribing (in one district alone, 63% of children who were young for their grade had been diagnosed), and she implemented a "positive discipline plan" that reduced ADHD behaviors. She also found that when teachers used these tools, students' standardized test scores dramatically improved.

LeFever Watson wasn't silenced forever; in addition to a bestselling book on how patients can advocate for themselves, she has also written articles on the skyrocketing diagnoses of ADHD in both children and adults. She contends that big pharma orchestrated this "epidemic" in collusion with some in the medical and insurance industries. Once a proverbial cry in the dark, she has in recent years been joined by others who believe that our children are being shortchanged to make adults' lives easier and pharmaceutical companies richer.

ADHD is the most studied pediatric mental health disorder. It first appeared on the radar in 1902, when English physician Sir George Frederick Still described children with "hyperactivity" and "impulsivity." More than a century later, ADHD has become a household word—it seems everyone either has a child with it or knows someone who does. The disorder even has its own awareness month—October.

In 2016, the theme for that month was "Knowing is Better," which is a bit ironic because it seems every new study or statistic only leads to more questions. We don't know exactly what causes ADHD, and there is still a debate about whether it's a social construct or an actual neurological condition. As there is no definitive test, some say it is often misdiagnosed, as was the case in Watson's research when she found that the youngest kids in the class were simply immature for their age.

The increase in diagnoses has sparked fiery debates among physicians, educators and parents, a growing number of whom are questioning why more of our children are being classified as "abnormal" and the efficacy—if not the morality—of relying on drugs to deal with it. One thing is for sure, the rise of ADHD—real or fabricated—is indicative of serious problems within the education system and our society as a whole.

In the 1970s, ADHD—"hyperkinetic reaction of childhood" as it was known back then—was a rare diagnosis (about 1% of school-age children were reported to have the disorder). The diagnosis was virtually non-existent for teens and adults. In 1980, the disorder, renamed Attention Deficit Disorder (ADD), first appeared in the Diagnostic and Statistical Manual of Mental Disorders (DSM-III). When DSM-IV was released in 1994, the disorder had been broken into three subgroups—combined, inattentive, hyperactive-impulsive.

In the 1990s, political changes and pressure from child welfare advocates resulted in ADHD being added to the Individuals with Disabilities in Education, which meant that children with this diagnosis were eligible for classroom accommodations. These are usually a combination of technological and simple, organic tools and are discussed in more detail later.

Since then, the number of people (children and adults)

being diagnosed with ADHD—and the prescriptions to treat it—has continued to climb with increasing (and to some, baffling) rapidity. In 2003, 7.8% of kids ages four to seventeen had been diagnosed with ADHD. By 2007, 9.5% had been diagnosed, and by 2011, 11% (more than 1 in 10 or 6.4 million kids) had been diagnosed. The number of prescriptions rose as well, from 4.8% of children prescribed in 2007 to 6.1% in 2011, an increase of 7% per year. Still, big pharma and its cohorts in the medical field have continued to claim that these drugs are "safer than aspirin." They also claim that the real problem is an under-diagnosis of ADHD and other childhood mental disorders.

The scientific and popular conceptions of ADHD have also changed thanks in large part to the Internet and social media. The DSM-5, released in May of 2013, further revised the information around ADHD to reflect current beliefs and in ways that some consider worrisome. Whereas the DSM-IV grouped ADHD under "disruptive behavioral disorders" like operational defiant disorder, the DSM-V has classified it as a neurodevelopment disorder, a grouping that includes Autism. This, along with some other changes, may partly explain for the increase in diagnoses of ADHD.

The indicators of ADHD include nine "inattentiveness" symptoms and nine "hyperactivity" symptoms. The inattentive symptoms include an inability to pay attention to details (including making careless mistakes), difficulty focusing on lectures or reading materials, being distracted when someone is speaking, difficulty following through on instructions (task completion), difficulty organizing, avoiding lengthy tasks (e.g., writing a longer paper), regularly losing things (e.g., wallet, phone, keys), distracted by extraneous stimuli, and forgetfulness.

The nine hyperactivity symptoms include fidgeting, leaving one's seat when sitting is appropriate or expected (e.g., in class), running around when inappropriate, inability to play quietly, excessive talking, interrupting others and/or calling out the answer to a question before the person has finished asking, overly animated as if "driven by a motor", and inability to wait in line.

These symptoms remain unchanged in the DSM-V. Furthermore, ADHD is diagnosed when children under seventeen show at least six of the nine inattentiveness and/ or hyperactivity symptoms. (For seventeen and older, only five symptoms are needed to diagnose because people tend to exhibit fewer symptoms with age.) Symptoms considered to be inconsistent with one's developmental stage must be present for at least six months.

That said, the bar has been lowered with regard to diagnosing ADHD. Whereas in DSM-IV, "some hyperactive-impulsive or inattentive symptoms that caused impairment were present before age seven," the DSM-V requires that "several inattentive or hyperactive-impulsive symptoms were present prior to 12 years." This opens up an additional five-year window for symptoms to appear. There is also no requirement that these symptoms impair functioning.

Also, the DSM-IV required that symptoms cause impairment in at least two environments (e.g., home and school). DSM-V requires only that the symptoms be present—again, no impairment needed.

While this explains, at least in part, the growing number of diagnoses nationwide, it certainly does not explain the wide variance in diagnoses at the statewide level. Nearly every state saw an increase from 2007 to 2011. For some, like New York, the increase was negligible (7.5% to 7.7%), while in Texas the percentage nearly doubled (4.8% to 9%). In a few states, the number of diagnoses actually declined; for example, New Jersey (6.9 to 5.5) and West Virginia (11.1 to 9.9), and in Alaska, the percentage held steady at 6%.

There are several theories about these discrepancies, including a lack of healthcare providers or Medicaid laws in a particular area and even the advertising for ADHD meds. Some studies have shown that sunlight eases the symptoms of ADHD and may even prevent it. Proponents of the theory point to the fact that Nevada has the lowest rate of ADHD in the country (4.2% as of 2011).

Psychologist Stephen Hinshaw and health economist Richard Scheffler, both of Berkley, suggest a very different, man-made reason for the wide spectrum of diagnosing and prescribing. Hinshaw and Scheffler began the research by looking at the extremes on either end of the spectrum and found that a child in Kentucky was three times more likely to be diagnosed with ADHD than one in Nevada, and a child in Louisiana was five times more likely to be prescribed medication. These were not out-liers either; the numbers were all over the chart. In fact, they noticed that states in the South had the highest rates of diagnosing and medicating, followed by the Midwest. In Kentucky, Arkansas, Louisiana, North Carolina, and Indiana, more than 10% of children had been diagnosed with ADHD, and more than 8% of them were prescribed medication.

On the other hand, states in the Northeast and the West had the lowest, with Nevada, New Jersey, Colorado, Utah, and Colorado consistently reporting that less than 5% of children had been diagnosed. This trend continued with regard to medication. Children with ADHD were less likely to be medicated if they were from Nevada, Hawaii, California, Alaska, or New Jersey.

After noting that the CDC had broken the country into ten regions, Hinshaw and Scheffler then looked at the commonly cited reasons for the prevalence of ADHD diagnoses and determined that, while each had some merit, none provided the connection they were looking for. They then circled back to the educational systems within these states. As in most cases, educators are the first to notice a child's symptoms. The results were both interesting and disturbing.

They found a direct correlation between high rates of ADHD diagnosing and "consequential accountability statutes," the most well-known of which is President George W. Bush's No Child Left Behind (NCLB). Essentially, these laws tie school funding to the passage of standardized tests. Other laws condition funding on proficiency exams, which high school seniors must pass in order to graduate.

When President Bush signed NCLB into law in 2001, thirty states already had similar statutes, some dating back to the early 1980s. Fifteen of seventeen Southern states had accountability laws, and thirteen of seventeen had the mandatory exams for graduating seniors. Hinshaw and Scheffler also found that poorer children were more likely to be diagnosed, which supports other studies on the relationship between socioeconomics and ADHD. These findings raised questions about the subjectivity of the diagnoses and the standards of the regional culture evaluating children's behavior as abnormal.

Schools in these states are highly motivated to diagnose their students. ADHD treatment improves school performance including test scores; it may also calm classroom disruptions, making it easier to teach the other students. Some states don't even factor in the scores of kids with ADHD when evaluating statutory compliance, which in and of itself is quite telling. If these tests are the primary means of gauging student success, how then are students with ADHD measured?

Hinshaw and Scheffler never claimed that ADHD is not a real disorder or that it does not need to be treated. They did suggest, however, that it is not always appropriately diagnosed and is often inappropriately medicated.

An increasing number of very young children are being labeled as having ADHD. In 2011, 237,000 American children aged two to five years had been diagnosed, a 50% increase from 2007-2008. According to the National Survey of Children's Health, that number reached 388,000 by 2016.

As if this wasn't complicated and frightening enough, it seems socioeconomics also seems to play a role in the number of diagnoses, or at least who is diagnosed. Kids covered by Medicaid are more likely to be diagnosed with ADHD than those covered by private insurance.

Within the Medicaid system, according to the CDC, foster care kids are three times more likely to be diagnosed with ADHD than those not in the system. Half of foster care kids also got a diagnosis of depression, anxiety or operational defiant disorder, compared with one-third of kids not in foster care.

While frightening, the rate of diagnosis in New York is below the national average (9.9% and 11% of children, respectively). A study from the CDC found that 10,000 toddlers nationwide are being prescribed meds, despite this being outside guidelines that favor other forms of treatment in children so young. Since the article appeared, other states had begun researching their own diagnosis and prescribing statistics. This leads to two questions: who is advocating for these children, and what impact will their "condition" and the choice of treatments for it have on the educational system?

As these statistics seem to suggest, the criteria for diagnosing ADHD is subjective and fluid, depending on where one lives and their socioeconomic status. Does that mean some of these children don't really have the disorder? There is a body of research to suggest that this is the case. One possible reason is that the person(s) evaluating them are rushing to judgment.

The child may be immature for his age or dealing with stressors that adults around him are unaware of. Another reason is that gifted children are being caught up in the ADHD net. Children with advanced cognitive and/or academic skills can behave much in the same way kids with ADHD do—their enthusiasm for learning is misinterpreted as "hyperactivity," and their inattentiveness is due to boredom because they already know what is being taught.

Other kids may be gifted and have ADHD, but educators and parents are often so eager to slap the ADHD label on them and thus reap the benefits of classroom accommodation that they overlook their natural abilities. These kids may have trouble focusing but may score off the chart in math or reading or be athletically or artistically talented. Regardless, as educators and parents, we should also be asking ourselves what we can be doing to support children so that they either avoid a misdiagnosis of ADHD or receive the appropriate treatment, which may or may not include medication.

To truly get to the bottom of this and break through the culture of complacency that has developed around ADHD, we must examine other possible explanations for its increasing prevalence. A 2013 article, after citing a CDC report of a 15% increase in diagnoses over the previous six years, pointed to studies regarding a decline in outdoor play (which they define as "on the grass," not cement) as a reason for hyperactivity and inattentiveness in children. These days, kids spend half as much time outside as they did before 1992. "Free play," or the organic games such as tag and hide and seek that many of us played with neighborhood friends, is virtually non-existent. Only 6% of kids spend time playing alone outside. Instead, they spend their time in daycare or school, their every moment carefully planned out by adults according to the latest fad or simply a lack of time. This is seen as a contributing factor to ADHD diagnoses, particularly in boys, as their ADHD typically manifests as hyperactivity and aggressiveness, whereas girls usually tend toward inattentiveness.

While ADHD and the decrease in free play are issues all over the world, it seemed the U.S. is leading the charge in the wrong direction. In Finland, children get seventy-five-minute recess periods. Japanese students get longer recess times plus ten to fifteen-minute breaks each hour. In China, kids don't necessarily get free play time, but they do get a morning exercise break when they stretch or run and another break when they move their eyes to music. In Norway, kids get outdoor play time regardless of the weather. Many of their school playgrounds have trees, and students are allowed to climb as high as they can. There are also rocks and sticks with which to build forts and whatever else they come up with in their imaginations. Perhaps most importantly, they are encouraged to solve disputes among themselves with little oversight from teachers unless it is necessary.

American children have on average one recess period lasting around twenty-seven minutes. This is a significant decrease from the 1980s when most young children got at least two recess periods. Schools have continued to cut down, saying they need more time for academics so that they can do better on standardized testing. Recess is often withheld as a punishment for bad behavior in the classroom and is decreased as children get older.

Playgrounds are viewed as "too dangerous," whether because of fear of "stranger danger" or fear of lawsuits. Instead, eight to eighteen-year-olds spend on average seven hours and thirty-eight minutes each day in front of some sort of screen (computer, TV, smartphone), not including the time spent on homework. Kids are often using these devices right up until they go to sleep, which suppresses melatonin and leads to delayed sleep onset and shorter sleep duration.

Scientists around the world have found that overuse of technology is causing significant, harmful physiological changes in both kids and adults. A study in South Korea yielded alarming results: one in five students were addicted to smartphones. They spent seven or more hours on them each day and experienced insomnia and depression when they were cut off. The screen time, they found, flooded the brain with dopamine and could lead to hypervigilance, aggression and overreaction to daily stimuli—hence the nicknames, "Digital Heroin" and "Electronic Cocaine." As noted earlier, natural light helps to counteract these effects, which may be a reason why ADHD diagnoses are less prevalent in states like Nevada and Arizona.

Whether a child is labeled ADHD also may depend on what country he or she lives in. In France, psychiatrists do not use the same criteria to diagnose conditions, though the symptoms of ADHD are the same. In fact, the DSM is so contrary to their view that in 1983 they developed their own system (the Classification Française des Troubles Mentaux de L'Enfant et de L'Adolescent) (CFTMEA) as an alternative to the DSM-III. The CFTMEA has been updated twice (in 1988 and 2000), yet it maintains that ADHD is not a biological condition but a psychosocial (situational) one.

When a child comes into their office, they adopt a psychopathological approach, meaning they look for the underlying reasons for the child's hyperactivity, inattentiveness or impulsivity—rather than rushing to label it. They ask questions about his/her home life (i.e., how are disagreements resolved at home? How much attention does he/she receive from parents? How does he/she relate to siblings?) The psychiatrist will also ask detailed questions about the child's diet to see whether he/she has any food allergies or is eating too many sugars or preservatives. This is a direct contradiction to the DSM, which simply checks symptoms off of a list without taking underlying causes into account. They also have a much wider range of what is considered "normal" childhood behavior.

According to a widely cited 2012 *Psychology Today* article, as of 2011, only 3.5% of French children had been diagnosed with ADHD. Since then, there has been major pushback, including several rebuttals in the same publication by people who cite the rate of diagnosis between 5.3% and 7.2%, which, if true, is still well below that of American children. The same people also claim that ADHD is vastly under-diagnosed. Sound familiar? They are singing the same tune of those who say it is under-diagnosed in the U.S. at 11%. It would be interesting to see a comparison between French and American children with the same symptoms, ten or twenty years out, to see how they are faring.

What is the reason for the different philosophy? Some cite the differences in the cultures, including more structured family life with things like meal times. There is also more of a focus on self-discipline.

Another important thing to note is a child's diet, which, as mentioned above, is taken into consideration by French doctors while evaluating a possible case of ADHD. While the FDA has stated that there is no definitive link between food preservatives and the disorder per se, it does acknowledge a correlation between certain food colorings and hyperactivity. In Europe, this link is taken much more seriously. In fact, many European countries have mandatory warning labels on foods containing certain colorings, stating that they "may have an adverse effect on activity and attention in children." Some of these countries, including France, have even banned the following:

Blue food colorings—these are found in things like brightly colored cereals, candies, chips, and yogurt;

Yellow food colorings—these are found in mac 'n' cheese, waffles, and cheese dips;

Red food colorings—these are found in cakes and frostings as well as more "benign" foods like oatmeal and yogurt.

In more recent years, American doctors have begun to include nutrition in their conversations with parents whose children are being evaluated for or diagnosed with ADHD. Coincidentally, the ideal diet is low sugar and processed foods which are likely to contain the food colorings mentioned above.

Bottom line: whether we buy into the French methodology

or not, don't we owe it to our children to investigate every possible alternative to diagnosing them with a "lifelong" disorder and probably pharmacological protocol? The next chapter will explore those protocols and explain how big pharma utilizes the culture of complacency to profit at the cost of our children's mental and physical well-being.

Chapter 4
Drugging Our Children

"I have absolutely no pleasure in the stimulants in which I sometimes so madly indulge. It has not been in the pursuit of pleasure that I have periled life and reputation and reason. It has been the desperate attempt to escape from torturing memories, from a sense of insupportable loneliness and a dread of some strange impending doom."

—*Edgar Allan Poe*

As mentioned in the previous chapter, ADHD is a two-pronged issue. It concerns not just the prevalence of diagnoses but the increasing number of kids being prescribed addictive, potentially harmful pharmaceuticals. Each year, more and more children are being medicated, some before they are even out of diapers, some without even an official diagnosis. As described below, this is largely a conspiracy between pharmaceutical conglomerates in collusion with cohorts in the medical and insurance industries, and often with the tacit agreement of educators and parents who are too busy to deal with children who do not fit into their strict parameters. This complacency is costing the American people not only billions of dollars each year but the health and vibrancy of future generations, the value of which cannot be measured.

There are two classes of drugs being prescribed to kids for mental health issues: methylphenidates (these include Ritalin and the less commonly known Concerta, Metadate, and Daytrana), and amphetamines (such as Adderall, Dextrostat and Dexedrine). While both types of drugs are central nervous stimulants that control the neurotransmitters dopamine and norepinephrine in the brain, there are some differences. Ritalin acts faster, peaks sooner, and lasts only two to three hours, while a dose of Adderall is active for four to six hours. Both types of drugs have had significant success in treating those with ADHD; however, the skyrocketing numbers of prescriptions, statistics about abuse and overdoses, and the lack of research on the long-term effects on young brains have many claiming that these drugs are less about making our children healthy and more about lining big pharma's pockets.

We can trace the rise in these prescriptions to the 1990s and the proliferation of studies on ADHD, most of which pointed to a growing pervasiveness of the disorder. To offset those costs, the healthcare industry looked to big pharma. Indeed, it seemed every trial also provided justification for meds, leading to a four-fold increase in prescriptions between 1987 and 1996. The late 1990s also brought a loosening in federal regulations about marketing these drugs; they could now be peddled directly to the public (e.g., parents of kids who "act out"). Suddenly, ads began appearing in popular magazines like

People and *Good Housekeeping*; they featured formerly out of control children now taking part in chores and excelling in school.

This, coupled with the FDA's Modernization Act, which extended patent exclusivity for new drugs, opened up an enormous new revenue stream for big pharma. Overnight, there was a flurry of research into a host of medications, including the methylphenidates and amphetamines prescribed for ADHD today. Drug companies also investigated new formulations and/or new uses for older drugs. Their efforts paid off to the tune of $9 billion, which is what these companies pulled in from ADHD drugs in 2012. This, according to data collection company IMS Health, was an increase from $1.7 billion just a decade earlier.

This was the case for Ciba, the Swiss pharmaceutical company that originally produced Ritalin in the 1940s. By 1956, it was being sold in the U.S. to treat severely depressed adult and elderly patients. Then, in 1963, two Baltimore researchers, Leon Eisenberg and Keith Connors, conducted a study of "disturbed children"—so labeled because they were, among other things, "disobedient" and "told lies." After Eisenberg and Connors determined that Ritalin was effective in controlling these behaviors, the FDA authorized its use for this purpose. It has been prescribed to American children ever since. Those numbers have continually increased, and regardless of the company's original motives, Ciba, along with other pharmaceutical companies, has been accused of marketing ADHD as much as the drug itself.

Today, Ritalin remains a highly controversial drug. On the one hand, it can help those with ADHD calm down, filter out distractions, and focus on the task at hand. Proponents of the drug also claim it prevents kids with ADHD from self-medicating with other substances when they get older.

Some studies show that kids with untreated ADHD are four times more likely to abuse drugs as adults; in fact, 10 to 30% of cocaine addicts have ADHD. On the other hand, there is a very real and growing concern that this is yet another epidemic orchestrated by big pharma in collusion with the health insurance industry and some medical professionals. There are even many parents who favor the pharmaceutical solution; they see Ritalin and other drugs as a "magic pill" that makes controlling their children easier at home, justifies accommodations at school and leads to better test scores and possibly admission to better colleges. This overreliance on pills, rather than utilizing organic behavioral approaches, is doing irreparable harm to future generations.

Those against the use of ADHD drugs claim that this overreliance on pills, often to the exclusion of organic behavioral approaches to ADHD, is doing children irreparable harm. They also claim that this overreliance is the result of a deliberate, well-planned campaign by big pharma. Their argument has several strong points, the most obvious of which is the increasing number of prescriptions.

Each year the Drug Enforcement Agency (DEA) publishes production quotes, and they are nothing less than alarming. In 1990, 600,000 American children were prescribed medication for ADHD, and despite the work of Gretchen LeFever Watson and others, that number has continued to climb. Between 2000 and 2005, there was a 9.5% increase in the number of prescriptions; and between 2007 and 2011, the DEA reported a 41% increase in ADHD stimulants dispensed in the United States. By 2013, 3.5 million children were taking medication for ADHD. Boys, who are two or three times more likely to be diagnosed with ADHD, were four times more likely than girls to be medicated for it.

Like the diagnosing of ADHD, the prevalence of meds depends on the region in which one lives. According to a 2003 report by the CDC, in California, 40.6% of children with ADHD diagnoses were taking medication compared with 68.5% of those in Nebraska. This, however, is not in and of itself evidence of overprescribing. Such evidence was found in North Carolina, however, where a study of eleven counties showed that 7.3% of kids were taking stimulants when only 3.4% had been given a neurological diagnosis.

While it might sound unbelievable that a child who has not even been diagnosed with a disorder may be prescribed a drug, it is actually an all too common occurrence. And, as mentioned earlier, a child's socioeconomic status often plays a factor in whether he or she is medicated. Kids on Medicaid are more likely to be prescribed medication for ADHD than those covered by private insurers. Foster children are also nine times more likely than others on Medicaid to be prescribed medication for ADHD and Operational Defiant Disorder, even though they comprise only 3% of the Medicaid population. This discovery prompted the federal Department of Health to write an open letter presenting Medicaid programs with new guidelines for prescribing mind-altering medications to children in foster care.

That letter came out in 2011, yet more recent studies indicate that these disturbing trends have continued on the state level. A 2014 article exposed the massive over-prescribing of Adderall and Ritalin for kids on New York State's Medicaid system. Concerned with a lack of data regarding ADHD meds and very young children, the state's Drug Utilization Review Board conducted an investigation. It found that 91% of kids covered by Medicaid and diagnosed with ADHD were taking meds, compared with the 67% statewide average.

But the truly appalling statistic was that 6,983 kids (9.2% of the 75,000 under seventeen on Medicaid) were being prescribed Ritalin and Adderall without a diagnosis! This included children two years of age and younger. At the time this article was written, the state had instituted new rules mandating that any prescription be accompanied by a diagnosis. However, this came only after a national backlash about these medications and pressure from child advocacy groups who contended that primary care providers were, to varying degrees, encouraged to diagnose and prescribe for ADHD even when they didn't know much about it. Advocates cited a shortage of child psychiatrists and the purported (and possibly exaggerated) long-term dangers associated with untreated ADHD. These dangers included increased risk of suicide, divorce and depression in adulthood.

Since then, federal U.S. health officials have also been advising parents of kids under the age of six to hold off on medication until they have tried non-medical therapies such as counseling and behavior modification. There is even an eight-week "boot camp" that teaches parents how to bond with their child and manage his/her ADHD-related behaviors. Those in favor of such treatments point out that there have not been enough studies on the long-term effects of ADHD meds on young brains and bodies. In the short term, they can cause insomnia, irritable mood, slowed growth, and poor appetite. In 2011, the American Academy of Pediatrics said the same, suggesting that non-medical options should be the first line of treatment for young children with ADHD.

Yet, despite these recommendations, less than half of children aged two to seven with ADHD were receiving these services, compared with 75% who take drugs. This has led many to wonder whether medication is more of a remedy for stressed-out parents than their children. Experts acknowledge that many lack the time and/or resources to engage in the behavioral work, which takes longer and more effort. It is also more costly since many private insurance companies don't pay for it. The benefits, however, can be much longer lasting than medication.

It is important to keep in mind that these statistics, as scary as they may be, only address children who are taking the medicine as directed. The medical com-munity maintains that they are at virtually no risk of becoming addicted, and while this may be true, abuse is nevertheless a severe problem, both by kids with legitimate prescriptions and those who have neither a diagnosis nor a prescription but acquire meds through "diversion" such as theft, sale or sharing. Most use them to lose weight or maintain focus through all-night study sessions, while others combine them with alcohol to achieve a high, which lends credence to the theory that ADHD drugs are gateways to abuse of opiates, including heroin.

The overprescribing of Ritalin and Adderall has made them more accessible; clever marketing as non-addictive "smart pills" has created the illusion that they are not as bad as street drugs when in fact they are close cousins. This is evidenced by Ritalin's litany of street names that range from the innocuous-sounding "Vitamin R" and "Smarties" to things like "Kiddy Cocaine." The same is true of Adderall, which is called everything from "Addys" and "Beans" to the more traditional "Uppers" or "Speed."

A 2012 study found that 22% of people diagnosed with ADHD exaggerated their symptoms to doctors, presumably to "score" a prescription for Ritalin and other drugs such as Adderall. It is unclear, however, how many of these people wanted the drugs for themselves or to dispense to others.

Indeed, the DEA classifies Ritalin as a Schedule II drug, along with codeine, morphine, opium, methadone, and oxycodone. It also has a chemical structure similar to that of cocaine and, when snorted or injected, delivers the same high at a much cheaper price. Like any drug, abuse of ADHD medications can cause horrific and even deadly reactions, including seizures, breathing problems, erratic heartbeat, and high blood pressure. Over time, such abuse can lead to stroke or mental issues such as mood disorders, hallucinations, paranoia, confusion, and delusions. There are also the inherent risks of injecting drugs including the spreading of HIV and other blood-borne illnesses. Ritalin can be particularly dangerous because of water-insoluble fillers that can block the user's blood vessels.

Ritalin can also lead to lifelong depression. It permanently alters the development of the brain, specifically, the "reward pathway"—the pleasure center that is stimulated by things like walking in a park or spending time with friends or a significant other. When the person stops taking these drugs, these natural highs no longer do the trick, and he/she is more likely to chase that euphoria with other substances. The risk is much greater for people who were misdiagnosed with ADHD or used the drugs to study or for recreation. Some studies show that adults who used to take Ritalin as kids are more likely to use cocaine. Moreover, 30 to 50% of kids in drug treatment centers have reportedly abused Ritalin.

Adderall is even more widely abused in the U.S. According to the organization Monitoring the Future, in 2008, 2.9% of tenth graders and 3.4% of twelfth graders abused methylphenidates. That number more than doubled when it came to Adderall and other amphetamines, with 6.4% of tenth graders and 6.8% of twelfth graders abusing them. In fact, these drugs ranked third for abused substances for twelfth graders that year.

A 2009 report released tracked calls to the American Association of Poison Control Centers from 1998 to 2005.

During those years, there was a 76% increase in the abuse of ADHD drugs, though it was not clear whether the increase was due to the number of prescriptions or the number of kids engaged in illicit use. Whatever the case, those who abuse the drugs are twice as likely to engage in criminal behavior, especially when they mix them with alcohol.

The dangers of misusing ADHD drugs have been known for years. In 2006, NBC news reported that 3,100 people go to the emergency room each year due to overdoses. However, it referred to them as "accidents" and said that at least two-thirds could be prevented if parents would simply lock them up. The FDA added a "black box" warning, its most serious, to the packaging for Ritalin, Adderall, and Concerta.

That same year, the National Survey on Drug Use and Health began reporting the number of people twelve and older who used Adderall for non-medical purposes such as weight loss, better focus, or recreation. They found that the number rose each year, climbing from 4.7 million in 2006 to 8.2 million in 2011.

A decade after that NBC report, the conversation dramatically shifted from accidents to intentional abuse, and with it the realization that the problem goes much further than parents and a locked medicine cabinet. A 2016 study released by the *Journal of Clinical Psychology* found that emergency room visits resulting from Adderall abuse went from 862 in 2006 to 1,489 in 2011—an increase of 67%. Most patients complained of anxiety, agitation, and insomnia, but there were some more serious cases, including heart attacks and strokes.

ER visits due to Ritalin abuse also increased, but as mentioned earlier, at a much lower rate. In 2011, Ritalin was responsible for 310 visits, up from 293 in 2006. Researchers attribute this in part to the fact that Adderall is an extended release drug, meaning the effects are steadier and last longer. This is helpful to students who want to stay up all night to study for finals or write term papers. Perhaps the most disturbing information to come out of the study was that college students using these drugs to enhance their academic performance believed these drugs to be harmless and more morally acceptable than others. Clearly, they were not educated about the consequences when they were younger.

As mentioned earlier, one of those consequences is a greater risk for abusing other substances. According to a 2017 study, ninety percent of those who had used Adderall for non-medical purposes were binge drinkers, and fifty percent were heavy drinkers. In the year prior to the study, Adderall abusers were also three times more likely to have used marijuana, eight times more likely to have used cocaine, five times more likely to have used painkillers, and eight times more likely to have used tranquilizers.

It is important to understand that this epidemic of drugging our children is not an accident, or "medical progress," but a meticulously planned and executed money-making operation by large pharmaceutical companies.

In December of 2013, a New York Times article exposed the many-tentacled approach of big pharma concerning ADHD diagnoses and medication in both kids and adults.

Keith Connors, psychologist and one of the two research-ers that spearheaded the landmark 1963 study on ADHD, has called the increase in diagnoses a "national disaster of dangerous proportions."

According to the CDC, ADHD is now the second-most diagnosed pediatric disorder after asthma. "The numbers make it look like an epidemic..." Connors said, "...it's preposterous ... a concoction to justify the giving out of medication at unprecedented and unjustifiable levels."

This was not merely the assertion of a disillusioned academic. Since 2000, the FDA has cited every major manufacturer for false and misleading advertising on ADHD drugs, including Adderall, Concerta, Focalin, Vyvanse, Intuniv, and Strattera.

Unlike most ADHD drugs, Intuniv and Strattera are not stimulants and carry a much lower risk of addiction; they've also been found to be somewhat less effective. Each has its own risks, including a litany of side effects ranging from nausea and vomiting to severe heart and liver problems.

Strattera, which is produced by Eli Lilly and Company, was approved by the FDA to treat ADHD after it was found to be ineffective as an antidepressant. In fact, it was discovered in a 2005 clinical trial that those taking Strattera are at a higher risk for suicidal ideation, resulting in a black box warning and an advisory for caregivers and teachers to keep a close watch over those taking it for disturbing changes in mood or behavior. In 2008, the FDA sent a warning letter to Lilly for false advertising, stating that it had exaggerated the benefits of the drug and minimized potential dangers.

Dr. Steven Webb

In September 2014, Shire, the company that produces Adderall, agreed to pay $56.5 million in fines for false advertising of Adderall XR, Vyvanse, and Daytrana, a patch that delivers the stimulant through the skin. Among other things, Shire had claimed that Adderall XR would "normalize" those with ADHD to the point where they would be "indistinguishable" from their peers who do not have the disorder. It also claimed that the drug, by virtue of controlling ADHD behaviors, would prevent criminal acts and sexually transmitted disease. These claims were unsupported by scientific data.

In 2016, Shire, who also makes Intuniv, was the subject of a class action suit. Plaintiffs claimed the company and its generic competitor intentionally dragged out the patent protection period, thereby preventing generic forms of the drug to enter the market and forcing consumers to continue paying top dollar.

Clearly, this was not the original intention of Roger Griggs, who developed Adderall in 1994 (under a different name and formulated for weight loss.) The company was later purchased by Shire for $186 million and repackaged it as a treatment for ADHD. Griggs has publically opposed marketing stimulants to the general public, calling such drugs "nuclear bombs."

Shire, on the other hand, has left no stone unturned with regard to marketing, all of which is geared toward making unruly children more manageable. In 2002, an Adderall ad showed a mother beaming lovingly at her son and saying, "Thanks for taking out the garbage!" In 2009, an Intuniv ad depicted a child pulling off a monster mask to reveal a sweet, happy face. The copy below it read, "You've got a great child in there."

The company has even marketed directly to children by funding 50,000 copies of a comic book that allegedly sought to destigmatize ADHD. "Medicines make it easier to pay attention," the superhero tells the kids, "and control your behavior!"

These companies have at their disposal an army of physicians that conduct research, consult with colleagues, and speak at medical conventions. The messaging is always the same: ADHD is underdiagnosed; the drugs used to treat it are helpful and safe; and, left untreated, people with ADHD will suffer severe consequences including but not limited to irresponsible sexual behavior, car accidents, divorce, and poor job prospects. This is despite the absence of evidence that long-term use of stimulants will prevent negative outcomes. Finally, they drive home the point that ADHD is a lifelong illness requiring lifelong medication, when, in fact, studies show that half of those who have ADHD as children are asymptomatic as adults.

These doctors are paid handsomely for their services, and the more prestigious their credentials, the larger the sum. One of them, Dr. Joseph Biederman, was affiliated with both Harvard University and Massachusetts General. He was also one of the most prolific researchers, writers, and advocates for big pharma, pushing their messaging not only for ADHD drugs but bipolar antipsychotics. "If a child is brilliant but just doing OK in school," Biederman remarked in a 2006 interview with Reuters Health, "that child may need treatment, which would result in their performing brilliantly in school."

In 2008, a Senate investigation found that his research was "substantially financed" by pharma, a fact Biederman conveniently forgot to disclose to either institution. He had personally made $1.6 million from his work on behalf of drug companies.

In addition to the doctors already in their pockets, the companies also directly market to other psychiatrists, pediatricians, and primary care physicians. Pharmaceutical reps regularly visit their offices to extol the virtues of ADHD drugs and downplay any risks. One Concerta ad read, "Allow your patients to experience life successes every day," while barely mentioning the disorder.

Big pharma has infiltrated every arena with regard to children's mental health. In 1987, Children and Adults with Attention Deficit/Hyperactivity Disorder (CHADD) was formed to inform the public about the disorder and dispel myths about Ritalin, the primary drug at the time. Several years later, CHADD began accepting money from Ritalin's producer, Ciba-Geigy. It also began distributing pamphlets that made the bold (and false) statement that "psychostimulants are not addictive."

The organization did not bother to disclose big pharma's funding until 1995 when it was exposed in a PBS documentary. Since then, they have revealed the names of their benefactors, including Shire, which gave them $3 million between 2006 and 2009. In return, CHADD agreed to distribute its bimonthly *Attention* magazine to doctors' offices. To this day, CHADD gets about $1 million a year, a third of their funding from big pharma.

The companies also give money to medical publications,

which in turn feature such ads as "Adderall XR Improves Academic Performance." From 1990 to 1993, the *Journal of the American Academy of Child and Adolescent Psychiatry* did not advertise ADHD drugs at all. A decade later, it was including one hundred pages of full-color ads each year.

Even the American Psychiatric Association (APA) receives large sums from drug companies. As mentioned in the previous chapter, the DSM, which is published by the APA, loosened the criteria for diagnosing ADHD to include things like "makes careless mistakes" and "difficulty waiting his/her turn."

Spurred by its success with children, big pharma has moved in more recent years to capture the adult market, which promises to be even more lucrative. They employ celebrity endorsements and online quizzes for adults to see whether they have the disorder or, as the companies' spokespeople claim, encourage them to speak to their doctor about the possibility. Often, the "symptoms" asked about in these quizzes can be readily explained by sleep deprivation and family and/or work stressors.

One particularly effective marketing tool has been to focus on the findings that ADHD is genetic. One pamphlet shows a family tree depicting all the generations who presumably have the disorder. This was despite the fact that most parents of ADHD kids are not afflicted. Shire produced a video in which a primary care physician diagnosed an adult male, whose son had already been diagnosed, in about six minutes. The doctor overseeing the creation of the video later backed away from it.

Given their extremely deep pockets and the many tools at their disposal, fighting these conglomerates can seem an unwinnable battle. However, in reality, it would not take too much to turn the tides. ADHD can be dealt with differently if more parents, educators, and other child advocates stopped burying their heads in the sand and insisted upon it.

No one is suggesting that ADHD is not a real disorder or that medication is never a viable option. That said, it is possible to stop the skyrocketing number of diagnoses and the prolific and unconscionable overmedicating of our children.

As mentioned in the previous chapter, France has other ways of dealing with ADHD, not only at the diagnostic phase but with treatment as well. Unlike the U.S. model, in which medication is still the primary—and sometimes only—method of treatment for ADHD, French doctors emphasize family counseling along with behavioral and nutritional therapies. Children are "prescribed" time spent in nature, bike riding, and changes to their diet. Drugs are rarely part of the equation.

In recent years, a relatively small but growing number of American doctors have started to take heed. While prescription drugs are still the go-to treatment, doctors are at least considering the potential benefits of counseling and behavior modification as well as supplements like iron, zinc and omega-3 fatty acids found in certain types of fish.

While most of the media attention has been focused on ADHD medications, there are a host of other meds being prescribed to our children. From 1993 to 2002, there was a five-fold increase in antipsychotic medication prescribed to children; antidepressant prescriptions increased three-fold between 1997 and 2002. The link between such medications and school violence will be covered in the following chapter.

That said, prescription drugs are not the only culprit; nor are they the only substances that, thanks to growing societal complacency, are becoming increasingly dangerous for kids. For decades, there has been a debate about whether marijuana is a gateway drug. However, whereas the majority of people used to say that it indeed led to harder drug use, the scales have now tipped the other way.

In recent years, marijuana has been touted as a cure-all for everything from anxiety to cancer. As of this writing, "medical marijuana" is legal in twenty-nine states, nine of which have legalized it for all adults over the age of twenty-one. Currently, a majority of Americans support legalization; in fact, it is one of the few issues today on which Republicans and Democrats can agree. In 2017, legal marijuana sales generated $9.7 billion in revenue.

The purpose here is not to dispute the benefits of marijuana or whether adults should be able to purchase it for health or recreation. Rather, the issue is marijuana's effects on kids, which has been shown to be anything but harmless. In fact, students who use pot have lower grades, impaired memory, and they are less likely to get into college. They are also much more likely to abuse other drugs. Marijuana used to be commonly acknowledged as a "gateway drug," yet now, thanks to aggressive marketing, society's complacency around youth and marijuana has grown apace with the argument for legalization.

Indeed, there are now a plethora of studies arguing that not only does marijuana not lead to harder drug use but it is actually harmless. These researchers contend that marijuana actually prevents usage of other drugs like heroin and cocaine—a similar argument made by proponents of medications prescribed for ADHD. Just as adults recognize the dangers of underage drinking, they need to understand that ignoring marijuana use is to contribute to the downfall of future generations.

The fact is, more than half of new illicit drug users begin with marijuana. This is not because the marijuana itself causes the addiction, but, like Ritalin, Adderall, alcohol, and even cigarettes, it rewires the brain, "priming" it to crave bigger and better highs. A study by the University of Michigan Medical School found that marijuana alters the dopamine receptors in the brain's reward system. This decrease in dopamine creates what researchers define as a "plateau effect," which means that when the high fades, the feelings the user was trying to escape are more intense. Kids are more susceptible to this, as their brains are still developing.

This is supported by statistics indicating that those who become addicted to pot are three times more likely to use heroin. Sixty percent of kids who smoke weed before age fifteen go on to use cocaine, and ninety percent of cocaine users began with cigarettes, alcohol, and marijuana. After alcohol, pot has the highest rate of dependence, with 4.2 million people identifying themselves as dependent as of 2013. This is twice that of prescription pain meds and five times that of cocaine.

There is another equally significant reason marijuana is a gateway for adolescents. Those who smoke pot tend to hang around other users, making it is easier to "score" it and other drugs regularly. They also fall prey to peer pressure and misinformation. For example, synthetic marijuana, which is made from a mixture of herbs and spices and sprayed with a chemical similar to THC, has been called "safe," "natural," and "legal." Nothing could be further from the truth. Users have no idea what chemicals are really used or whether it has been sprayed evenly. They are basically experimenting with an unknown quantity.

At the time of this writing, the Illinois Department of Health had just issued a warning about synthetic cannabinoids after two people died and fifty-six others in the Chicago area were hospitalized for "severe bleeding." Medical tests revealed that nine of those people had ingested an ingredient commonly found in rat poison, and after finding that the products were bought in convenience stores as well as from dealers, the Department called it a "public health crisis" and urged people not to use products bought within the previous month.

It has been found that these synthetic cannabinoids, which are designed to give the user the same effect as the real thing, are much less predictable largely because those creating it consistently change up the chemicals used in order to circumvent the law. Synthetic marijuana is an issue across the country, including California, wherein

2016 governor Jerry Brown expanded a 2011 statute making such products illegal. The expansion covered such chemical alterations.

The important takeaway here is that the substance abuse epidemic would not be possible without the cooperation of parents, educators, and doctors. The word "cooperation" is used not to attribute nefarious motives to them but rather a combination of miseducation and, yes, complacency around children's well-being.

Teachers understandably want to be able to manage their classrooms without distractions. Parents want to feel that their children's behavioral issues can be handled so their sons and daughters can live up to their full potential. Perhaps they even want to believe that in a dangerous world, marijuana is an innocuous, even beneficial substitute for alcohol and other drugs. That is not the case, however, and parents cannot afford to bury their heads in the sand. The time is long overdue for those who care most about kids to take back their power from media talking heads, pharmaceutical corporations who care only for the bottom line, and bureaucrats whose focuses are on standardized test scores rather than finding the best organic tools for educating our youth.

CHAPTER 5
Children Under Attack

"What we must do now is enact change because that is what we do to things that fail: we change them."

—*Lorenzo Prado, Parkland Shooting Survivor*

On May 18, 2018, Sabika Sheikh entered Santa Fe High School, never in a million years imagining that she would soon meet her death. The seventeen-year-old foreign exchange student from Pakistan had, according to her host family, wanted to positively impact the world. Instead, she became one of countless young people to die in one of the mass school shootings that are occurring in this country (and around the world) with increasing frequency.

Dimitrios Pagourtzis, also seventeen and a fellow student, walked in with a shotgun and a .38 caliber handgun and embarked on a twenty-five-minute shooting spree, killing eight students and two teachers. Thirteen others were wounded. Each time he shot another person, Pagourtzis allegedly said, "Another one bites the dust."

Detective Reice Tisdale, Jr. arrived on the scene to help, only to learn that Cynthia Tisdale, his mother and a substitute teacher at Santa Fe, was one of the dead. In a culture where school violence had become far too common, these personalized accounts are what stick in people's minds once the dust has settled.

In the investigation that followed, most students who knew Pagourtizis described him as a "quiet" boy and did not consider him a threat, but his social media posts tell a very different story. These include a picture of a "Born to Kill" T-shirt and a black duster with Nazi, communist, religious and fascist symbols in a jumbled code only he understood. There were also reports that Pagourtzis also aggressively pursued classmate Shana Fisher. A week before the shooting, Fisher, who was also killed, had very publicly turned him down. There has been speculation as to whether this was the motive, but so far, it remains a mystery.

While writing this book, it was hard to keep up with the horrific school shootings taking place around the country—from Florida to Texas, Virginia to Kentucky.

On January 23, fifteen-year-old Gabe Parker walked into Marshall County High School with a handgun, killing two students. Eighteen others were injured either from gunfire or in the melee that ensued. Everyone in this tight-knit community of 4,500 was shocked but no more than local reporter Mary Garrison Minyard, who arrived to cover the story and learned that her own son was the shooter. Parker said he was conducting an "experiment."

For Christina Hadley Ellegood, a paralegal in nearby

Paducah, Kentucky, the news brought up horrible personal memories. Twenty years earlier, Ellegood's sister was shot and killed by Michael Carneal, a fellow student at Heath High School.

I also vividly remember that day. It was Monday, December 1, 1997, and I was just twenty-seven years old and the principal of a small school in rural southern Illinois. The school, which housed a middle school and a high school in one facility, had around two-hundred students. I was also the boys' varsity basketball coach and the athletic director. This combination of job duties certainly was atypical but not unheard of.

I had just returned to my office after my morning rounds—complete with high-fives and small talk of what the kids did with their weekend—and was about to start sifting through unopened mail and disciplinary referrals from the week prior. Suddenly, I heard a commotion in the office and people running, then the sounds of sobbing. Most of the words were indistinguishable, but I could clearly make out, "Oh my God! Oh my God!"

I jumped up and ran to the door. At precisely the same moment, one of my junior high teachers met me at my door with a look of pure terror on her face.

"Oh my God!" was all she could muster as she grabbed my arm. Then, with short gasping breaths, she uttered the words that both terrified me and clarified my work as an administrator: "There's ... been ... a ... shooting!"

At that moment, visions of a school shooter on our campus and the possible actions I would have to take to stop him raced through my mind.

"There's been a shooting at my son's school!" she screamed. "I've got to go!"

By this time, all of the secretaries, the school guidance counselor, and the school superintendent, who was also housed in our facility, had entered the small hallway just outside of my office to investigate the commotion.

So scared was I at the thought of an active shooter that it took a minute to realize the teacher was asking permission to go find out if her child had been shot, or worse.

I remember saying, "Go" several times, then the whole group of us walked with her to the door in a show of support. My own two children were very young at the time, and all I wanted to do was call home to see if they were okay.

The teacher was still screaming, "Oh my God! Oh my God!" as she left the facility and hurried to her car. We all just stood there shocked and silently hoping for the best.

I still couldn't shake the thought of the shooting occurring at our school. Once her car was out of sight, we began the process of debriefing what had just occurred and what information we could find that could explain the situation. Soon enough, we found the story on a local news station.

At 7:05 a.m., fourteen-year-old Michael Carneal entered Heath High School in neighboring Paducah, Kentucky with a rifle, a shotgun, and a handgun and did the unthinkable. He went to the school with the sole purpose of ending as many lives as he possibly could. He walked up to a prayer group and, using the handgun, opened fire, killing three students and wounding five others. My teacher's child was at the school but was unharmed.

Paducah is a beautiful town nestled near the banks of the Ohio River, just across the river from my school. We share beautiful forests and widespread southern hospitality. We have small rural schools where the tight-knit communities and undeniable pride in our mission drives our success. How is it that a child, barely a teenager, could even have such thoughts of destruction and mayhem, let alone bring them to fruition in such a bloody and brutal fashion?

This was not a pedophile—known to target children. This was not a recently paroled violent offender determined to unleash his festering rage upon society; nor a "gangbanger" hell-bent on revenge or entering some "revered" social group by way of a senseless slaughter. This was not any of the sandman characters we lie awake in fear of at night, hoping and praying they never darken our doorstep or lurk in the basements or any other cold, dark area that typifies the fears and concerns we have as humans. This was a child killing another child. A child whose first words to the principal upon finishing the last round in his handgun were, "Please kill me. I can't believe I did that!"

Carneal, who had passed his blanket-covered rifle off as an art project, couldn't give authorities a motive, though later he would say he thought his parents didn't love him. He had also allegedly been bullied by other students who falsely accused him of being gay. Carneal was sentenced to life without parole for twenty-five years. In 2002, five years after the shooting, Carneal told a reporter, "People want one simple answer—I can't give it."

As with any post-crisis, we begin with a picture of the perpetrator, placing blame through "what went wrong?" assessments and end with "what could we have done to prevent this?" discussions. Were there signs? What was going through his head? Did anyone know he was capable of doing this? These are questions for which there are no answers. The "after the fact" discourse is only there as a predictor of certain behavior—certain cause and effect sociology. What drives us as humans is that we believe that someone should have known this was going to happen. Someone is to blame. Should the parents have known? Yes. Should the school have known? Absolutely. Is a gun-friendly society to blame? Most assuredly. Is there anything or anybody else out there you would like to blame?

That is the easy part, you know—blaming that which is tangible and can be entered into the equation as a socially accepted effect following cause. The truth is, research and all of the couches in the psychiatry profession in and of themselves will not help us overcome the challenges we must confront in our schools on a daily basis. Interacting with human nature and the desire to measure and find some sort of success is the key.

People want to be successful in life. It is as involuntary as hunger pains. Finding out what "success" a person is striving for is the end-game. Michael Carneal showed signs of "not normal." I use the term loosely, for as a school administrator, I believe the term "normal" is irrelevant;

all kids are different. Hence, all kids are "normal" … until they are not. Michael Carneal had behavior that was "normal," and some that may be reasonably considered abnormal. He attended public schools for years and consistently adhered to school rules. He wanted to date girls that he liked. He also covered vents in the bathroom because he thought he was being watched.

Enter abnormal.

This is certainly something that would make an administrator give pause and thought to something that was more than just "weird"; but lest we forget, that was not against school rules. I know of no school that has a policy against covering vents in a private bathroom. So, is this now a sign of a killer? Is that the breakthrough we were looking for? Are we now adding the bathrooms as a common denominator to predict school violence? I would suggest that we are not.

There is no checklist of indicators that we can use at the school door threshold to determine which one of our students is going to try to find their version of success at the end of a weapon. We are the gatekeepers, but how do we know who to allow through the gates? Who are we going to deprive of their "free appropriate education" as demanded in federal statutes? After all, we are educators.

Although it occurred more than two decades ago, Carneal's response was one we should pay close attention to. In the wake of such a tragedy, everyone wants a decisive answer for why the perpetrator acted, preferably one that vindicates their actions.

For example, after a May 2018 shooting in Santa Fe that left ten people dead, Texas Lieutenant Governor Dan Patrick blamed violent video games for desensitizing our children to violence. As we will see, however, there is never just one reason for these incidents but rather a combination of factors that, combined with a lack of preparedness, create the perfect conditions for a tragedy.

Given the number of school shootings plaguing our national consciousness, it may be difficult to believe that school homicides have actually declined since the 1990s. So why does it seem hardly a week passes without hearing of another horrific scene? As we will see, there are a number of reasons for this. One of which is because the killings prevalent today are not committed in the heat of the moment over a pair of sneakers (though these obviously troubling incidents are nothing to be dismissed) but premeditated and planned out in great dramatic detail, right down to the shooter's clothing, choice of weaponry, and declarations of political or social philosophy.

April 20, 1999 began like any other day in Littleton, Colorado, with springtime fragrances and beautiful mountain ranges. Although the mornings carry a slight chill, they hardly warrant the wearing of trench coats. But such a coat is certainly no indication that one is a killer, or at least it wasn't that day.

I am describing the moments just before to the infamous Columbine High School shooting, where two teenage killers descended upon unsuspecting high school children and slaughtered them as they crouched beneath their desks. Were the shooters "weird" in the eyes of a gatekeeper? Was there something about them that should have triggered our sixth sense of self-preservation? Eric Harris and Dylan Klebold were children. They played video games and enjoyed fantasy. They also amassed several handguns and long guns and constructed ninety-plus bombs to be used to kill their peers. History will always be judged by the "what ifs," and we are still assessing and studying the events that led up to such a tragic event.

Many now emulate shooters who have gone before them, holding them up as idols or martyrs, particularly Eric Harris and Dylan Klebold. For example, nineteen-year-old Alvaro Castillo, who on April 30, 2006 killed his father before shooting two students at his former high school in North Carolina, wore a trench coat similar to those of Harris and Klebold. Unlike many shooters, Castillo did not take his own life but surrendered without incident. As he was led away by law enforcement, he shouted, "Columbine! Remember Columbine! Eric Harris! Dylan Klebold!"

Beforehand, he had made a series of videos, including one in which he said, "It's time to teach history a lesson." While reasonable minds can debate what he meant by this statement, it is clear that he believed he was in fact making a profound statement in word and deed. He was righting some sort of injustice.

Castillo was but one example of the "anti-hero" persona adopted by many school murderers. This persona, seen in countless films from *Rambo* and *Dirty Harry* to *The*

Matrix, is a favorite in American culture; it symbolizes the sort of flawed but courageous individual who rises above his circumstances to change the status quo. Most of us see this as harmless entertainment. A troubled, marginalized youth, however, sees it as a call to action.

Seung-Hui Cho, who on April 16, 2007 killed thirty-two people and wounded twenty-five others at Virginia Tech, also appeared to have adopted this persona. In between the two separate attacks launched by Cho that day, he went to the post office and sent a package to media outlets. Amongst the materials were Cho's manifesto, in which he stated his hatred for the rich and compared himself to Jesus. He also referred to the Columbine shooters as "martyrs."

Cho, who from childhood had been diagnosed and treated for depression, anxiety and other mental disorders, had been accused of stalking two female students two years prior to the shooting. Yet, thanks to legal loopholes, he was permitted to purchase the Glock 19 and Walther P22 he used to carry out the killings. It is, to date, the deadliest school shooting in U.S. history.

There have been almost three hundred attacks since the Columbine and Virginia Tech events, yet these remain prevalent in the school violence discourse. Dylan Klebold and Eric Harris were just everyday high school kids who'd had enough of the bullying and spent well over a year devising a plan to get even—a plan that included martyring themselves.

Children who are experiencing what I have coined "The Cynosure Effect" are always thinking of ways to become

"Instafamous." Cynosure is the act of "getting all eyes on me." Klebold and Harris had talked about this and devised plans and obtained weapons for the sole reason of turning everyone's attention to them. And the fact that current and potential murderers can "relate" to them shouldn't just turn our stomachs; it should be the primary research results we are constantly searching for. Humans stoke passion when there is a revolution against wrongdoing.

The approach to preventing school mass murders must be two-pronged. One is getting to the root of the problems causing our youth to murder their classmates, teachers and parents, and the other is to protect the physical structure of the school. Both require that we replace our culture of complacency with one of vigilance, compassion, and commitment to not simply graduating our children, but helping them to become well-adjusted, self-realized adults that realize their value individually and as part of our society. Indeed, this is the only way we will save our society.

The question is, how do we begin to tackle this multifaceted crisis with all its moving parts? I have been known to say, "To understand your parameters is to understand your plight!" I meant this not only literally (i.e., protecting the parameters of the school building and grounds) but figuratively as well. In other words, the way we frame the problem of school violence is often tying our hands in trying to solve it. Our guiding principle, therefore, must be a willingness to look at and operate from reality, not the quagmire handed to us by the media, bureaucrats and politicians.

Let's first take a look at the some of the scapegoats; these apply not only to the types of school shootings we see today but other acts of violence dating back decades. While these things may contribute to social ills, they are not, as some would have us believe, the real underlying cause. This is evidenced by the fact that attempts to regulate and legislate them out of existence have failed miserably.

A popular scapegoat today is video games, particularly "first-person shooter games," where the player steps into the shoes of the person holding the gun. These have long been cited as having an unhealthy effect on young minds. Indeed, Eric Harris and Dylan Klebold were known to play these games, as well as other perpetrators of school mass murder. In 2015, the American Psychiatric Association determined that these games lead, or at least contribute, to an increase in aggressive behavior and a decrease in empathy for others.

This blame game is nothing new. Anyone around in the 1980s will recall the vilification of heavy or "death" metal music as a cause of teen suicides. It has even been the subject of litigation. In 1990, two Nevada families brought suits against CBS Records and the rock band Judas Priest, claiming the band had embedded subliminal messages in the music that drove their sons to suicide five years earlier. Though the existence of such messages had yet to be determined, the families' lawyers argued that they would be outside First Amendment protection.

On December 23, 1985, eighteen-year-old Raymond Belknap and twenty-year-old James Vance shot themselves in the head with a 12-gauge shotgun. The two had spent six hours drinking beer, smoking pot and listening to Judas Priest, then apparently made a suicide pact and headed to a church playground to carry it out. Belknap died instantly, and Vance sustained horrific injuries to his face requiring numerous surgeries. He became a born-again Christian but eventually started using drugs again and died three years after the first attempt. Before his death, he specifically blamed the music for "mesmerizing them" and making them "tired of life," hence the pact.

Both the band and the record company were charged with the manufacture and marketing of a faulty product, as well as negligence and intentional and reckless misconduct. If the plaintiffs were successful, record companies would have had to screen lyrics or leave themselves open to further suits and huge sums in damages.

"Judas Priest and CBS pander this stuff to alienated teenagers," the lawyer for Mr. Belknap's family stated. "The members of the chess club, the math and science majors don't listen to this stuff. It's the dropouts, the drug and alcohol abusers. So our argument is you have a duty to be more cautious when you're dealing with a population susceptible to this stuff."

Indeed, both Belknap and Vance would be considered "susceptible." Both families had a history of domestic violence and child abuse and had received counseling. They had also dropped out of high school and had criminal records and difficulty keeping jobs. Yet, their parents chose to focus on the music rather than the drugs, alcohol, and other issues as a source of their suicide attempt. As with other cases involving Ozzy Osbourne and other heavy metal singers, the judge found that Judas Priest was not liable. Yet, to this day, this music genre is considered poisonous to youth. As a society, we continue to focus on the outside influences instead of getting to the root of the problem.

Heavy metal is apparently not the only culprit musically speaking. In 1992, Steven Stack of Wayne State University and Jim Gundlach from Auburn University published a report connecting country music with higher suicide rates. Their study, which focused on whites living in forty-nine metropolitan areas, found a direct correlation between radio airtime devoted to country music and local suicide rates.

"The effect," Stack and Gundlach contended, "is independent of divorce, southernness, poverty and gun availability." Instead, their analysis of 1,400 songs in this genre determined that three-quarters of them lamented about romantic loss, financial challenges, and loneliness. The overall tenor was one of hopelessness. Furthermore, alcohol was depicted as a necessary tool for coping with life's problems. For those already at risk, listening to these songs can push them over the edge.

An even bigger issue is our focus on the tools used in the attack. By this, I refer to the ongoing gun debate in this country, which is highly politicized and a distraction from what is really causing these incidents. As we will discuss later, the media is an incendiary force in this debate.

For example, CNN has reported that the U.S. averaged about one school shooting a week in 2018, perhaps in an effort to stir up the gun control controversy. That is not the intent here; while everyone is rolling around in the mud, our kids are getting killed. That said, if we want to stop school shootings, we must understand our true adversary, and it is not guns. The Gun Control Act was enacted in 1968. Since then, gun laws have become increasingly stricter, most notably after school shootings such as Sandy Hook. Yet, school shootings have continued to increase, from seventeen over the entirety of the 1950s, to sixty-two between 2000 and 2009, to the one hundred forty-plus since 2010.

If guns magically disappeared tomorrow, the problem would still exist. We all know the saying—where there's a will, there's a way. If nothing else, these school murderers all have a very strong will. If they cannot get the job done with a gun, they will use something else. To know the truth of this, we must only look at the recent spate of terrorist attacks, one in which the perpetrator plowed a vehicle into a crowd of pedestrians. They are able to accomplish the same objective—causing deaths and instilling fear—without the complications of bomb-building or securing weapons.

The same is true of school attacks. On October 24, 2011, a fifteen-year-old girl in Snohomish, Washington attacked April Lutz and Beckah Staudacher, neither of whom she knew, in the bathroom of their high school. Lutz, who was stabbed twenty-five times, nearly died three times on the way to the hospital. Staudacher was stabbed in the arm when she tried to protect her friend.

In the aftermath, it was discovered that six months earlier, the attacker had told the school counselor that she had violent thoughts that included killing her own mother and brother as well as another schoolmate. "I get these really like sick thoughts of killing people, and it's not just like shooting someone I hate," the girl said, according to the counselor's records. "It's like sick, twisted ways of the people I love. And the thoughts keep getting worse. It's not normal, is it?"

The girl was suspended and sent for evaluation, but just ten days later, the hospital deemed her "safe to return to school and home." The high school let her back in, and she continued therapy for the next several months. She was also taking psychotropic drugs.

At some point, she had sent a classmate a message saying, "One day I am going to snap and kill everyone." And snap she did; Lutz and Staudacher were simply at the wrong place at the wrong time. The victims' families were later awarded a $1.3 million settlement for failure to protect their students. The perpetrator is currently serving a thirteen-year sentence, first at a juvenile facility, then a women's prison once she turns twenty-one.

In 2014, sixteen-year-old Chris Plakson stabbed fourteen-year-old Maria Sanchez to death just hours before their prom. His reason: she had declined to be his date. Plakson, who had been taking prescription meds for ADHD, followed her into the stairwell of their Milford, Connecticut high school and plunged a steak knife into her neck and check. He pled no contest and was sentenced to twenty-five years.

As these two examples make clear, gun control is not going to solve the problem of school murders. This is not to say that legal loopholes allowing mentally ill people to purchase guns should not be closed; merely that if they cannot obtain a gun, they will find another way to carry out their plans. Such political debates are a distraction from the real issues and perpetuate the culture of complacency around violence. They have us fighting each other about politicized issues when we should be working together to build schools that foster creativity and inclusiveness.

Again, this attempt to legislate our troubles away is nothing new. At the time of this writing, a New York federal court overturned, on Second Amendment grounds, a 1974 state statute banning the possession, use, and disposal of nunchaku, or "nunchucks"—a potentially lethal weapon comprised of two rods connected by a chain.

James Maloney, a professor at the State University of New York Maritime College and an amateur martial artist, challenged the law in 2000 after he was charged with having nunchucks in his home. He apparently wanted to teach martial arts, including the use of nunchucks, to his twin sons. The case went all the way to the U.S. Supreme Court, which upheld the ban. However, in light of another Second Amendment decision, it later sent the case back for reconsideration by the lower court. The federal judge found that the Second Amendment right to bear arms extended beyond guns, thus ending Maloney's eighteen-year fight.

What is pertinent here is the reason the law was enacted in the first place. Back in 1974, martial arts films, particularly those of Bruce Lee, were very popular. Lee was often seen whipping around his nunchucks, and lawmakers believed this might lead to a rise in "mayhem" among youths influenced by Lee. One need only Google crime statistics in New York City to see how ineffective this ban was, as criminals will use whatever is at their disposal. The thought that a person intent on breaking the law might abide by such a ban flies in the face of logic.

Ironically, such attempts to regulate violence out of our society do not extend to pharmaceuticals, which, as discussed earlier and researched thoroughly, are being prescribed to our children at an alarming, ever-increasing rate. The link between prescription medications and school violence dates back more than twenty years.

The Citizens Commission on Human Rights, which has been monitoring school violence since 1999, reported that SSRIs are listed in the Top Ten Drugs that cause violence; this is why they have had "black box warnings" for years. Amphetamines are 9.6 times more likely to be linked to violence than other drugs. Strattera, which was mentioned in the previous chapter, is commonly prescribed for ADHD, carries a significant risk of suicidal ideation and is, in fact, nine times more likely to be connected to violence.

Nikolas Cruz, who, in early 2018, killed seventeen students and teachers at the Marjory Stoneman Douglas High School in Parkland, Florida, was also taking meds for ADHD, depression, and autism.

In fact, in 2016, his compliance around taking his meds and showing up to therapy appointments was cited as a reason for not hospitalizing him. Henderson Behavioral

Health was called in to evaluate him when Cruz, then a student at the school, made a Snapchat video in which he cut his arms and said he wanted to buy a gun. After conducting an evaluation, which was bolstered by the statement of Lynda Cruz, his adoptive mother, that he did take his meds and did not have a gun, the facility released him over the concerns of the school's counselor. Florida Children and Families was also alerted and similarly found compliance sufficient to let the matter drop.

This one fact—his medication—apparently overrode the massive amount of evidence that this young man was a danger. After the shooting, it was revealed that approximately thirty people knew of his threats of violence, history of torturing animals, and expressed desire to commit an act of violence at school. Some did nothing; others did voice their concerns and went unheard. Even the FBI neglected to follow up after receiving a tip about Cruz.

As far back as 2015, he carried a bag with a Nazi symbol and made derogatory remarks about African Americans. Cruz had also made a series of videos in which he stated, "You're all going to die. I can't wait," and, "With the power of my AR, you will all know who I am." This was a reference to the AR-15 rifle that he would later use in the shooting.

Before her death in the fall of 2017, his mother, over the strenuous objection of the school, had allowed him to purchase guns. The neighbors who subsequently took him in kept those guns locked away. They said they had no idea how he gained access to them or that "a monster" was living in their house. While his mother's behavior constitutes enabling at the very least, there is little doubt that this highly disturbed and motivated young man would have, in the absence of guns, found another way to carry out an attack.

At the time of this writing, Nikolas Cruz is waiting to hear whether he will face the death penalty or life imprisonment. Now the focus is not on Lynda Cruz but his biological mother, Brenda Woodard. A career criminal and drug addict who has served time in jail, she gave Cruz and his brother Zachary up for adoption shortly after their birth. She also admittedly smoked crack while pregnant. Cruz also has a half-sister Danielle, who is currently in jail for attempted murder among other things.

His lawyers are hoping this abysmal family history will persuade the jury to spare his life. Whatever the outcome, there is no doubt that the system failed this young man and, by extension, those he eventually killed. Focusing on the fact that he carried it out with a gun only distracts us from the myriad of other factors that contributed to this tragedy. Since then, new legislation has been passed mandating mental health plans in schools. Ironically, Henderson Behavior Center, the same facility that released Cruz, has been chosen to partner with Florida charter schools.

Cases like Cruz also shine a light in the role of the media in this distraction and likely the propagation of copycat attacks. If one goes on the TMZ website, they will find a profile of Nikolas Cruz under the "celebrity" tab. It is not just tabloid news either but mainstream news outlets such as CNN and *The New York Times* that use these crimes in their scramble for relevancy.

As in every school massacre, Cruz's face was plastered all over the airwaves for weeks. Reporters dissected his life, his proclivities for violence, and how he compared to other shooters. In doing so, the media acts as a proverbial match to the flame. Why is this? Because such coverage goes to the very heart of what causes these attacks in the first place: the killers' desire for fame and a place in history. As the videos and other writings of mass murders show, they blame others for their problems and fantasize about settling the score.

Dr. Park Dietz, one of the country's foremost forensic psychiatrists, has been a vocal opponent of such coverage. Over his decades-long career, Dietz has consulted and/ or testified in some of the highest profile cases, from O.J. Simpson and the Unabomber to Jeffrey Dahmer and Columbine. He concluded that, while each school murderer has his own set of issues and life events leading to the attack, they all have this need for fame and notoriety.

The media feeds this desire by covering attacks in great detail, analyzing (and, some would argue, glamourizing) every aspect of the shooter's life. This may seem appealing to disempowered youth who feel invisible and discounted in their daily lives.

As Dietz stated: I have repeatedly told CNN and our other media, "If you don't want to propagate more mass murders, don't start the story with sirens blaring. Don't have photographs of the killer. Don't make this 24/7 coverage. Do everything you can not to make the body count the lead story and not to make the killer some kind of anti-hero. Do localize the story to the affected community, and make it as boring as possible in every other market. Because every time we have intense saturation coverage of a mass murder, we expect to see one or two more within a week."

Tom and Caren Teves, whose son Alex was killed in the 2012 theater shooting in Aurora, Colorado, created No Notoriety, a campaign imploring the media to be more mindful of the way that it covers such incidents. In short, the campaign asks that they report the name and likeness of the individual only after the person is first identified, the exception of course being if the person is still being sought by law enforcement. They should also refrain from showing all the videos and manifestos made by the killer and instead focus on the lives of victims. They should share the analyses of mental health and public safety officials with a goal of preventing mass murderers. In other words, they should place the need for public safety (i.e., the risk of encouraging copycat attacks) above their desire for ratings.

So far, their appeals, as well as those of Dietz and other healthcare professionals, have fallen on deaf ears.

As mentioned previously, the media also frames the conversation about these murders oftentimes in keeping with a political agenda. Race also appears to be a factor in the way such crimes are reported. For example, an urban school shooting in which the shooter and/or victims were African American will warrant a much shorter report and with an underlying tone of "this is just life in the big city." When the shooter is white and in a suburban or rural setting, however, there is a tenor of "how did this happen here?" which of course adds to the salaciousness of the story. In doing so, the media is not simply informing us of the facts but attempting to set an agenda that may or may not have as its goal the end of these attacks.

In order to really begin to deal with school violence effectively, we must look at the true cause, which is primarily social rejection and/or bullying. As children are growing and seeking acceptance, they suddenly feel isolated from others and like they are on the outside looking in. Many school murderers see themselves as victims, either of their individual circumstances, society as a whole, or both.

As Seung-Hui Cho said in one of his videos, "You forced me into a corner and gave me only one option." It is not clear what perpetrators he was referring to or how he felt that they boxed him in, but his statement is a profound one.

A 2014 study found that bullied students were twice as likely to bring a gun to school, and though in most cases they are seeking not to hurt others but to protect themselves, it still makes for a volatile situation. Clearly, we need to stop focusing on the political debates and media sensationalism and instead focus on how we as a society are boxing our children in. To do this requires us to take the blinders off and address the larger issues and our own culpability in them.

CHAPTER 6
The Culture of Connectedness

"The life I touch for good or ill will touch another life, and that in turn another, until who knows where the trembling stops or in what far place my touch will be felt."

—Frederick Buechner

Throughout this book, we have discussed the culture of complacency dominating our educational system and the horrific effects this culture has had on our children and our society as a whole, particularly the increasing number of school massacres. Each of these attacks leaves us with a choice: mourn the dead and lament more peaceful times, or take the actions needed, not to go back to yesteryear but forward into an environment that nurtures and empowers future generations. If we choose the latter, we are agreeing to wage a battle on two fronts: addressing immediate threats to our kids' safety and putting long-term measures in place so that they do not feel so desperate to begin with.

Compare, for example, the Parkland shooting—in which numerous people including Cruz's mother, peers, and healthcare professionals allowed his violent ideations to fester—with the following:

On March 23, 2017, administrators at Catoctin High School in Thurmont, Maryland received a frantic phone call from a man who believed that there was a credible threat against the school. The alleged perpetrator was his daughter, honor student Nicole Cevario. He had found her journal outlining a highly detailed bomb plot that included a "to-do" list and her intention to kill herself by gunshot. There was also a receipt for the shotgun, which she had purchased legally (at the time there were no background checks in Maryland). Apparently, she had been planning the attack for about four months, and "D-Day" was just a few weeks out.

Nicole was immediately and without incident removed from class and taken for psychiatric evaluation. A subsequent search of her room uncovered bomb-making materials. In addition to her high school work, Cevario had been taking criminal justice classes at the local college and held down a job at a local restaurant. Now she is in prison, serving a twenty-year sentence after pleading guilty to possessing explosive material with the intent to create a destructive device. It is a waste of life to be sure, but, thanks to her father's actions, it pales in comparison to the carnage Nicole had planned.

While we do not know the extent of her motives, Cevario expressed a desire to become the first female school shooter. "By definition," she wrote, "a school shooter has to be attending the school they target at the time of the attack, and I haven't found a single woman who has fulfilled that criteria. Guess it's meant to be me. Yes, I know it's meant to be me. This is what I'm supposed to do. Maybe not with my life, but with my death."

She also referred with some reverence to the attacks at Columbine, Colorado and Sandy Hook while at the same time dissecting the shooters' mistakes and stating how she would do things better. Indeed, among her notes, authorities found the information she had collected on the school's emergency procedures and the movements of the school resource officer. Oddly, however, she identified committing suicide as her primary goal. The murder of her classmates and teachers was her "Plan B."

"It just really hit me this afternoon," Cevario wrote. "I realized I was going to die surrounded by people I hate in a building I hate."

It is not clear what led Mr. Cevario to discover the journal. He saw that something was off and chose to follow the breadcrumbs. That does not mean it was easy for him to do. One can only imagine the agony and inner turmoil he and his wife felt before and after making that call. It is never easy to admit that our children are troubled let alone capable of such a heinous crime, but to do otherwise is to sentence them to a life of torment and possibly imprisonment and/or death, not to mention the fate of their victims and the impact on society as a whole.

The Cevarios exhibited the type of courage needed if we are to make real, sustainable change. Stories of thwarted attacks coupled with more responsible reporting of those that are carried out will eventually lead to a decrease in copycat massacres, or at least it won't encourage them.

A joint study by the U.S. Secret Service and the U.S. Department of Education examined thirty-seven school attacks occurring between 1974 and 2000. They concluded that ninety-eight percent of perpetrators had experienced a recent loss or failure (for example, Dimitrios Pagourtzis being snubbed by the girl he was interested in), ninety-three percent had planned the attacks in advance, and eighty-one percent had explicitly revealed their intentions. This means that, while we probably cannot stop all attacks, we have an excellent chance of stopping a good portion of them.

Let's break this down. First, in every case described in this book as well as countless others, the school murderer had for some time been on someone's radar due to a history of mental health and/or behavioral challenges. When that person then experiences a loss or failure (for example, the death of Cruz's mother), this constitutes another red flag, signaling to teachers, parents and others that this child needs additional support, evaluation, surveillance, and perhaps hospitalization or incarceration.

The second and third components go hand in hand. As we have seen, many of these kids have a social media presence, and they are not shy about using it to voice their opinions. They talk about what they want to do and why they want to do it. Others tell guidance counselors and sometimes even peers. This is why it is so important to get other students to speak up when they see anything troublesome such as a Facebook post, tweet or video. As kids may be hesitant about being considered a "snitch" or the current term "OP" (operative), we need to be clear that we are enlisting them to safeguard their safety and that of their friends. We make them a part of a courageous and critical process. Just as important is to make sure adults listen to their concerns and take immediate and decisive action, be it notifying law enforcement, sending them for psychiatric testing, and so on.

Some high schools are already using companies to police social media sites for threatening posts. This has become one of those politicized distractions mentioned earlier. While some support such surveillance (in fact, schools have been sued for not monitoring such posts), it has met with some resistance from the ACLU and others who argue that it violates students' First Amendment rights. Sometimes, kids need to "vent," they say, it is not the same as acting out. They forget that there are exceptions to free speech, including "hate" speech or words that incite violence. If a Snapchat video declaring a commitment to Nazi ideology and a desire to kill one's classmates does not fit into that exception, nothing does.

Our job goes far beyond preventing the next attack, however; it is about creating an inclusive environment where all kids, regardless of their background, appearance, academic and athletic abilities, feel like they are both individuals and part of something greater than themselves. In short, they are learning to be well-adjusted, productive members of society. For this to happen, we need a massive shift in the way we approach education in this country.

Needless to say, this is an extremely tall order. As organizational research specialist Margaret Wheatley stated in 1999, "We live in a society that believes it can define normal and then judge everything against that fictitious standard." She added that our future lies in institutions based on principles and relationships rather than simply rules. Nowhere is this more apparent than in our educational system.

The No Child Left Behind Law was quite possibly the most detrimental thing to happen to children since the federal government became more involved with K-12 education in the 1960s. It approaches schools and the process of schooling with a "one size fits all" mentality that leaves little to no room for individuality.

Schools, and by extension our children, are judged on the basis of rigid test scores, which places an incredible amount of pressure on teachers to deliver. In order to combat the social isolation that leads to depression, anxiety and, as we have seen, violence, we need to define success for students with multiple metrics including individualized plans.

In an ideal world, each child would receive the sort of personal curriculum mandated by law for special education students. With the question "What would connect this student to school?" foremost in their minds, teachers, parents, and guidance counselors should at the beginning of each school year sit down with the student to assess his/her strengths, challenges and interests.

The goal of these interviews should be to find out what makes them tick, what they are passionate about and good at, and create a plan based on that. The rest of the year should be spent building on this connection with regular follow-ups to check in on their goals and their progress in reaching them, making adjustments as needed. There should also be a transition plan in place to take effect when the child turns sixteen. This plan requires an honest assessment of the best path for him/her.

Not every kid needs to be shepherded into college. One need only look at the job situation for millennials to see that. We instead need to re-examine the vocational trades that can lead to fulfilling and lucrative careers. We need to be nurturing their natural creativity rather than forcing them into a neat little box based on our own often misguided image of what constitutes "success."

Additionally, children who have experienced traumas such as abuse, negligence, and poverty need extra love and care, not the added stress of cookie-cutter academics. For students with ADHD or other challenges, there are many simple, organic methods to help them learn. For example, if a child is distracted by goings-on outside the window, the teacher can seat them in the middle of the room. If he/she does not respect personal space, their desks can be moved further apart. If a child is becoming distracted, a private personal cue that brings him/her back to the present can be established. If they are restless, the teacher can give them errands that allow them to move around or, if possible, let them stand while doing their work, or give them short breaks between assignments.

Another option is to give them instructions in written and oral form and ask the student to repeat them back, out of earshot of other students to avoid humiliating him or her. Above all, these children should be included in the lessons as much as possible to create a feeling of inclusiveness and connectedness.

For their part, parents must, to the best of their ability,

provide structure with regular bedtimes and meals. This can be difficult for those who work as the evenings are often the only time they have to spend with their children. The goal here should be to achieve a balance that allows both time for parent and child to bond while giving them the best possible chance to succeed at school.

It is time that those administering those academics should think of themselves less as "teachers" and more as "mentors." It is time we stop telling students what they need to learn and start helping them find information that broadens their passion for knowledge. If a child is looking for knowledge, they will find it almost immediately.

Children are ignited by a revolution as well, and years of watching children morph into adults have made one thing very clear—the advent of technology has exploded this desire for attention and this insatiable need for a cause. If you want to research, watch a group of kindergartners walk into a classroom with their newest iPhones. Ask them questions and let them ask SIRI and watch how quickly their eyes light up with information. THIS is eye-opening, cutting-edge research. THIS is our world.

We also must realize that our work does not end with the school day. Enjoyable activities, programs and services can help kids make invaluable connections and hopefully foster feelings of acceptance and community. Gangs are not simply the color-bearing, inner-city warriors we see on television and in films; they are groups that provide that acceptance and protection albeit at a high cost that includes criminal, overly violent behavior. These groups may not be as noticeable in suburban and rural areas, but they exist all the same, and if we do not claim our children, rest assured they will. We need to find activities that kids like, or will like, once they get involved. For example, in the rural school I live near, I suggested starting a bass fishing program. Why? Because everybody can learn to fish, and I wanted those kids who were not necessarily athletic and/or were academically challenged to have a part in something—to connect with something. My goal is always to get one hundred percent of our students involved in an extracurricular activity sponsored by a caring adult, so that instead of finding a "hang out," they find a "hang in" in a positive atmosphere with people who have their best interests at heart.

Clearly, this undertaking is not for the faint of heart. It also requires every tool in our arsenal, including technology. This can be a tough pill to swallow for administrators who have seen the worst aspects of the "information age." Indeed, much of this book has focused on how the internet, particularly social media, facilitates bullying, spreads hateful ideologies, and even glamorizes mass murder. The truth is, used properly, technology could provide incredible support both academically and socially.

For example, there is an app called inClass, which records the lecture as the student takes notes on a device. The app syncs the notes with audio, both of which can be referenced later on and digested at the student's pace. Students can also use a smartphone or watch app to vibrate at certain intervals, which helps them keep track of time. Technology is also, to some people's chagrin, here to stay, so we may as well make it our friend.

As mentioned earlier, video games, specifically violent ones, have been cited as a disturbing commonality among school murderers; they also potentially contribute to a lack of empathy. Even non-violent games have become controversial in that they involve even more screen time in an already overly digital world.

While these arguments certainly have merits, and I would never advocate that children, troubled or not, play extremely violent games, I would point out that there are several benefits to playing age-appropriate games. They improve hand-eye coordination and manual dexterity; in fact, a study showed that surgeons who played two to three hours per week made thirty-two percent fewer errors during practice procedures.

Playing these games also helps those with dyslexia—reading comprehension was improved following gaming sessions—and strengthened eye muscles for those with "lazy eyes," even to the point of normalization. Gaming can also ease physical pain by refocusing one's attention and ease cravings such as smoking and overeating.

Gaming fosters leadership skills, faster decision-making, and critical thinking. Also, as many are set in different time periods, they can provide an informal history lesson. It also enhances memory and multitasking skills. And, as odd as it seems, it can lead to physical activity. For example, a child may enjoy playing basketball or canoeing in a game and decide to take it into "real life."

Finally, and perhaps most importantly, gaming encourages personal connection, both with in-person players and opponents online. Gamers are less likely to bully, in part because playing both the hero and the villain gives them greater awareness of the effects that the bad guys' actions have on others.

As we have seen in this chapter, there are several methods we as administrators, teachers and parents can employ to decrease school massacres in our country as well as make school a more fulfilling, individualized experience. The following chapter will address the weaknesses in our physical parameters—our school structures—and how we can correct them.

CHAPTER 7
Time for Change

"You may say I'm a dreamer, but I'm not the only one. I hope someday you'll join us, and the world will live as one."

—John Lennon

Throughout this book, we have discussed the myriad of challenges facing our children today, from bullying to drug addiction, from the ever-increasing number of diagnoses of mental illness and behavioral disorders to the (over)prescription of pharmaceuticals and the school violence that often occurs as a result. We have also discussed what school administrators and other stakeholders can do to mitigate these challenges so that students grow up to be productive, well-adjusted members of society.

However, even if we do everything right, there will be those who slip through the cracks. And of those, there will be some who plan and attempt to execute an attack on a school. There are still others, whether they be disgruntled teachers or terrorists, homegrown or foreign, who want to do us harm in furtherance of a personal, religious or political motive.

Bottom line: emergency situations will arise, and we must be prepared to deal with them in a way that minimizes casualties. To do anything less is a grave disservice to our children, our communities, and our society as a whole. In this chapter, I will cover the potential weaknesses in the physical structures of our schools and what we need to do, both to prevent such an attack and to respond should one occur. Again, the biggest barrier we face is our own culture of complacency that tells us, "Those things just don't happen here."

In February 2016, four years and two months after Adam Lanza's horrific school shooting that killed twenty children and six adults, the new Sandy Hook elementary school opened. The design of the fifty-million-dollar building is not only beautiful, with a rainforest and study spaces made to look like tree houses, it is also fitted with subtle but state-of-the-art security measures. The goal and challenge were to prevent another atrocity while fostering a welcoming environment conducive to learning.

The concept was not just the brainchild of a brilliant architectural team, though it clearly was that, but the result of an ongoing collaboration with stakeholders including local and school officials, members of the governing board, and neighborhood parents and teachers. It is now being held up as the new standard in school architecture, a blend of beauty and functionality for our dangerous, 21st-century world.

Indeed, every detail of this new facility was contemplated with security in mind, including its landscaping. First, the school was built on raised ground, which allows employees to see who is approaching the school while making it difficult for potential perpetrators to see inside the classrooms. Second, the architects used the natural environment, positioning parking lots and drop-off areas around wetlands and ponds. This allowed them to direct visitors to new pedestrian bridges, then through two sets of security doors before entering the school.

There is also a long walkway through the rain garden, which makes a quick escape difficult and reduced visibility from the street; the design even controls how the traffic flows around and up to the school in order to allow early detection of threats.

Dickinson Drive, the road leading to the school and the one used to evacuate the survivors of the massacre, now has several checkpoints including a surveillance gate and main entrance. The building is also buffered by a bus loop and layers of parking.

Inside, the classrooms are far from the entry points, and each has a security door and lock. There is also hardened glass in the sidelights, capable of withstanding ballistic-level force; the walls are hardened as well. The whole building and the grounds have been fitted with a state-of-the-art surveillance system. Nobody is getting in or out of that building without administrators and law enforcement knowing about it.

To the inexperienced eye, it is a stunning structure surrounded by lush greenery. To those who participated in its creation, however, it is a vow that the events of December 14, 2012 will never be repeated.

As Sandy Hook first selectman Pat Llodra said, "Let me state unequivocally that we would trade in a minute this beautiful new school for the more familiar and ancient Sandy Hook school, built in the '50s, if we could just change the past."

While this sentiment is certainly understandable, we no longer have the luxury of wishing for bygone days. Dawn Hochspring, Sandy Hook's principal at the time of the shooting, knew this.

Earlier in 2012, Hochspring had installed a security system that identified visitors and automatically locked the doors at 9:30 a.m. This did not deter Lanza, however, who used his AR-15 to shoot out the window next to the door. Within minutes, he had already killed Hochspring and Mary Sherlach, the school psychologist. Staff who heard the gunshots immediately followed security protocols, but once Lanza had gained access, it was too late. The psychological and emotional devastation to the parents, surviving children and staff, and the community is far-reaching and incalculable.

Sandy Hook is by no means the only example of vulnerabilities in the physical structure and/or security protocols. Nikolas Cruz, the shooter in Parkland, Florida, entered the campus through the gates surrounding the school, which were open so buses could collect students at the end of the day. Indeed, the Monday morning quarterbacking done after every attack reveals areas that could have been better protected, safety plans that could have been in place, and things that could have been done differently.

We cannot continue to wait until a massacre happens before revamping a school. The question then becomes, what can we do to build safer schools and better secure the schools we have now, particularly in areas that have funding issues?

The increasing numbers of mass shootings have revolutionized the field of architecture, particularly with regard to schools. The concept of functionality now goes far beyond facilitating the business of the structure (i.e., learning and sports) to include how to deter, detect and thwart threats of all kinds. For example, landscaping, even simpler than that used in Newtown, can be utilized with bushes and trees placed around the perimeter to make it more difficult for an attacker to approach the school quickly. This also allows staff and security to spot an attacker's approach and commence with security protocols.

Architects are now taking their cues from other high-value targets like banks, where the goal is to have all those entering and exiting clearly visible to staff. This technique is called "layering," and in schools, it includes not only doors but the hallways as well; both should be situated in a way that they can be locked or closed off from the rest of the building in the event of an active shooting or another type of attack.

As Jim Childress of Connecticut-based firm Centerbrook Architects stated, "There should be layers of zoning. Even if the intruder gets past the front entrance, and students can take shelter in different areas, so the intruder has a hard time moving through the school itself."

Of course, not every school district is considering, or can afford, to build a new building. However, there are several improvements that can be made to existing structures to either reduce the chances of an attack or make it easier to defend against one.

One such improvement is so-called "safe rooms." In the 1950s, schools throughout America were outfitted with "fallout" or bomb shelters in which students and teachers could take refuge in the event of a nuclear attack by the Soviets. Safety protocols were created around the threat, including regular "Duck and Cover" drills. Without warning, the teacher would yell "Duck!" and the children would know to drop to the floor and cover their head and neck with their hands. Anyone who theoretically survived "the blast" would then go into the fallout shelter to wait out the radiation.

Thankfully, this never happened. The point here is that they were diligent about preparing. Flash forward to today, the threat of shootings or other attacks is much more likely, yet many of us still believe it is not going to happen.

That said, many architects are now incorporating "safe rooms" into the designs of new schools. Similar to the fallout shelter, it provides a secure area that staff and students can flee to when there is an active shooter on campus. These rooms are locked from the inside and made of concrete, so even the bullets of an automatic weapon cannot penetrate. These rooms can also protect from acts of God. For example, schools in the Midwest, particularly Oklahoma, have such rooms where people can go for shelter during a tornado.

Even safety rooms are not sufficient, for as we've seen in Sandy Hook and many other shootings, people will not always have time to make it there. Sandy Hook also exemplifies the vulnerability created by having regular glass windows. That's why the new building and many other schools are opting to replace the windows with bulletproof glass or other alternatives.

The problem here is financing. Many school districts, especially those in impoverished areas, will not be able to spend the estimated twenty-five to one hundred dollars per square foot for this type of window. Regular, single-pane glass only costs about three dollars per square foot.

As Jim Childress stated, "I don't know any public schools that could afford that, so it becomes society's question." Indeed, what are we as a society willing to give up in order to keep our children safe?

Another measure that can be used to improve an existing building is adding walls and fences around the periphery. Some schools have shied away from this option because, unless the wall or fence is designed in an aesthetically pleasing way, it can give a school a prison-like appearance. Again, it often comes down to finances; even without the extra expense of a high-end architectural firm, walls and fences can be quite costly, especially if the school hires an armed guard to man the fence.

Every school, old or new, should be outfitted with a foolproof alarm system. Ideally, there should be one main entrance that is under constant surveillance. Given fire concerns, this will not likely be the case, but any and all other exits should be armed with a working system that is always monitored by staff and linked to local law enforcement. Furthermore, these doors should only be able to be opened from the inside.

There have been cases when alarms have been disconnected from police stations due to the cost associated with false alarms or pranks played by students, but this is simply unacceptable. If pranks are an issue, institute strict consequences such as suspension, detention or charging parents a fine (in fact, newer systems are now able to indicate to administrators whether there is really a fire even before the rest of the school is alerted). But the most important thing is that law enforcement be made aware of an attack as soon as possible.

In Hermiston, Oregon, police are now mandated to respond to every fire alarm in the event that there is an active shooter or some other type of attack. This is in response to the Parkland, Florida shooting, during which Nikolas Cruz pulled the fire alarm to get more students and teachers into the hallways and in his sights.

At the time of this writing, Florida is considering a new bill that would mandate silent "panic" alarms linking all public schools to local law enforcement. The proposal is called "Alyssa's Law," after fourteen-year-old Alyssa Alhadeff, who was killed by Cruz.

If it passes, every building on public elementary, middle or high school campuses would have to have at least one panic alarm for situations unrelated to fires, including active shooters. First responders would receive a signal as soon as somebody activated the alarm and, more importantly, before the 911 call is even made.

Alhadeff also inspired a similar bill in New Jersey, where her family lived before moving to Florida. Unfortunately, after five years of consideration, that state has yet to enact such a measure.

We don't only have to worry about students. What about a teacher on a rampage, opioid addicts, and homegrown or foreign terrorists with political or religious motivation? We also need to address the possibility that weapons other than guns, knives or bombs can be used. For example, how well are we protecting the school's food supply from being tampered with? Are we securing air louvers to make sure someone cannot use them to introduce a poisonous gas or biochemical weapon into the school?

Before Timothy McVeigh bombed the Alfred P. Murrah Building in Oklahoma City in retaliation for ... we couldn't conceive that an American would do such a thing. Before September 11, 2001, we couldn't conceive that men use airlines to topple some of our tallest buildings and decimate the Pentagon. Given all that has happened in the world since then, we cannot feign such ignorance when it comes to our schools or any place where children, our most precious resource, are gathered in one place.

One must only look to the Beslan massacre to realize the truth of this. On September 1, 2004, thirty-two members of the militant group Riyad-us-Saliheen attacked a school and took 1,200 people hostage. Their goal—Chechen independence and the withdrawal of Russian forces from that area. The group was known for its suicide missions, and indeed, the hostage-takers wore suicide belts and placed bombs in the school gymnasium. During the three-day siege, more than three hundred thirty people were killed, roughly half of them children.

If your first reaction while reading this was that it happened "over there," or in a dangerous part of the world, know that this is precisely the sort of complacent thinking that we must seek to eradicate from our hearts, minds and policies. Consider this: even if a group like Riyad-us-Saliheen does not attack a school, they are actively trying to recruit our kids. Terrorists have access to the same news we do. They see the obscene amount of media coverage we give mass shooters, and they know their profile: the lone wolf who is already in our school hallways and classrooms.

As previously mentioned, these kids want desperately to "belong" and to prove their power over others. They also often have access to weaponry and perceives perpetrating such an attack to be his greatest glory. Add to this the ready-made political or religious agenda and "justification" provided by terrorists, these kids are ripe for the picking.

These and other horrifying situations beg the question, how do we dismantle the culture of complacency around the threats to our schools and come up with real 21st-century solutions? To answer this question, I turn in the next chapter to The PARA Mindset, which I have developed as a result of my decades in facing these threats head-on, both in law enforcement and as a school administrator who has seen far too many children fall through the cracks. The PARA Mindset is named for the prefix "para-" which derives from the Latin "to shield."

PARA comprises four overlapping steps—Preparation, Awareness, Responsiveness, and Advocacy.

CHAPTER 8
The PARA Mindset

"If you change the way you look at things, the things you look at change."

—Wayne Dyer

Changing our mindset to protect children is grounded in and supported by the Social Systems Theory, which regards a stable social group as a coherent whole composed of a myriad of relationships between individuals, groups, and institutions. It envisions a school contained in a physical place, within a strong barrier (exo-system); composed of distinct, connected spaces (each one a micro-system) through which students pass every day; and situated in a larger community of stakeholders (macro-system) whose laws and culture empowers the management of the school. The PARA Mindset is much more than just an acronym for some type of response to a violent situation as society continuously craves. If we change our way of thinking, we increase the capacity for changing how the system operates as a whole.

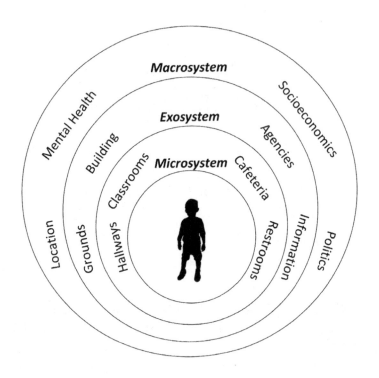

The PARA Mindset is the 21st-century framework for making schools safe. It is about consistent, situational awareness. Rather than dictating a list of rules, PARA supplies a formula for applying these principles to your existing relationships and in building new ones every single second that you interact with children and each other at school.

PARA's guiding principles are:

- Prevention is the goal. Safety plans must eliminate or neutralize as many threats as possible (e.g., the doors are checked every morning).

- Safety is infrastructure. Safety can be engineered into the campus, the school building, and every zone within the school. As I like to say, "Know your perimeter, know your plight."

- Safety is an educational matter. Every child deserves to be safe in school and deserves to provide input on how to keep the school safe.

- We must build alliances between stakeholders. School officials, families, law enforcement, social work agencies, and mental health providers need to share information that affects school safety.

- Every adult—parent, teacher, resource officer, or school administrator—has a role in the safety plan (e.g., every teacher has a walkie-talkie). The day-to-day implementation of that role must be second nature.

- Funding matters. It matters for facility design, for delivering appropriate educational programs from special education to vocational education to STEM, and for hiring qualified staff and giving them ongoing training. This is how we build "connectedness," connecting the child with something they appreciate.

- One size doesn't fit all. Research has shown that local, site-based management teams know what's best for the children in their care and must be empowered to make decisions. (In the state of Illinois, school boards have final authority.) What works in Manhattan, population 1.6 million, won't work in Goreville, Illinois, population 1,067.

- Educators have a duty to inform themselves, to instruct parents, and to advocate for legislation, research, and nationwide standards.

THE PARA MINDSET

PREPAREDNESS AWARENESS

RESPONSIVENESS

ADVOCACY

Preparedness

I liken the culture of complacency in this country to a disease, and preparedness—defined as "the state of being prepared"—as the only cure. In the context of schools, preparedness is relative to the efforts of the institution and the social networks that make up the larger organizational system.

To better illustrate systemic preparedness, it is helpful to look at the operation of an engine. If a portion of the engine is not working properly (for example, if not all of the pistons or spark plugs are prepared to accept the influx of gas, and only a portion of the pistons are able to perform correctly when the gas is introduced) the vehicle may be able to trudge along for a while, but failure, whether it's when the vehicle tries to climb a hill or swerve to miss something in its path, is inevitable.

The same is true of a school's organizational system that lacks collective preparedness. Yes, most schools have some sort of protocols for dealing with a violent event or some other type of trauma after it has occurred, just as most have trainings that discuss the importance of being prepared to deal with school violence. However, there is a difference between talking about preparedness and actually being prepared to deal with such an event at a moment's notice.

In fact, research suggests that after news of a school shooting breaks, educational institutions—usually at the teacher and administrator level—will enhance their preparedness activities for approximately thirteen days before slipping back into their pre-event, this-can't-happen-here mentality.

This culture of complacency is the primary cause of the lack of preparedness needed to make our schools and other soft targets (e.g., churches) safe. If teachers were told that there would be an event in their classrooms tomorrow, I would suggest that every last one of them would be prepared to address that event. Systemic preparedness is the same concept: everyone prepares as if the event IS going to happen tomorrow.

To better explain the insidious nature of the culture of complacency, I have divided the concept into three distinct stages: the "Sigh of Relief" Stage; the "Disengagement" Stage, and the "Degradation of Duties" Stage.

During the "Sigh of Relief" Stage, the teachers and school leaders are—in addition to empathizing with the victims and thanking God that it didn't happen at their school—still identifying potential threats in their own environments. At the same time, however, they are also noting that students seem to be adjusting to what happened, due in part to all those school safety training videos and new protocols that were introduced at the beginning of the school year. School must and will go on after all. This is where the danger begins anew.

As time passes—and, given the "normalizing" of such violence in today's society, this can be a matter of weeks—school administrators and teachers slip into the "Disengagement Stage." They are still somewhat diligent in locking the doors and identifying potential threats within their classrooms and immediate area, but they begin to display overconfidence that they can handle any possible threat. Thoughts of school safety begin to fade into the background rather than being front and center as they were immediately following the event. Therefore, less effort is taken to prepare the students and the environment for potential violence.

Lastly, during the "Degradation of Duties Stage," teachers and school leaders become set in their ways—consumed by the routine of coming to the school, opening the classroom, teaching the subjects, and dismissing their students until another day. They fail to notice subtle changes and warning signs in the environment around them, which, by definition, is a state of unpreparedness or complacency.

During the investigation following the Challenger disaster in 1986, researchers found that, over time, there was a profound degradation of standards, which they called "normalization of deviance." In an educational setting, this means that as teachers and school leaders go about their daily routines and become less diligent regarding school safety practices and procedures and nothing happens as a consequence, the new routine becomes the standard practice.

As former Senator Orrin G. Hatch of Utah once said in an interview regarding post-crisis complacency, "…we're an optimistic people in this country, and we generally believe we're going to be alright, and that's what we want people to believe…."

True as this may be, there is a fine line between being

"optimistic" and burying our heads in the sand. Indeed, in order to increase the likelihood that our kids will be "alright," schools, communities, and quality leadership must ensure that we inoculate our educational environments through constant and consistent school safety measures and ideas.

To summarize how to maintain "preparedness," there are three main areas to address:

- Work with ALL stakeholders to develop emergency management policies and procedures.

- Provide quality training in ALL areas of preparedness—NOT just response during and after an attack.

- Conduct quality drills and exercises often and all-inclusive of the system as a whole.

First, in order to encompass all stakeholders, you must identify the stakeholders, including teachers and students at ALL grade levels. Gone are the days where we isolate children from decision-making. For better or worse, they are, thanks to social media, already far savvier than we give them credit for; therefore, to exclude them from the decision-making process not only marginalizes them but also eliminates a valuable resource we need to make schools safer. Of course, I am not suggesting we provide students with training on stopping shooters as is often sensationalized in mainstream media. I am referring to gathering student input on social issues and pitfalls that adults who did not grow up in this era have little knowledge of. We must educate and protect the children we have today, not who we think they should be based on yesterday.

Other stakeholders include school social workers, guidance counselors, municipal leaders, community faith groups, parent organizations, library foundations, and so on—any individuals or groups that make up the fiber that holds the institutional system in place.

These groups are essential, not simply as resources to tap for quality information around policies and procedures but because they offer an opportunity to utilize groups who are not in the daily routine of educating children. In other words, they are outside the culture of complacency, educationally speaking, and can therefore potentially offer outside-the-box suggestions. These organizations can carry the message of preparedness to their prayer groups, the city council meetings, and so on, thus creating a ripple effect of awareness throughout the community.

Secondly, most trainings for schools and school personnel center upon responses to some type of crisis. While response trainings are important, we also need trainings for 21st-century challenges, such as trauma-informed mentoring, "stop-the-bleed" and other medical information, and other "lessons learned" trainings from mistakes made in the past. Training teachers to be great educators is more than just making sure they are current on the subjects they cover in class; it is about taking them out of their comfort zone and preparing them to help children survive and thrive in a violent world.

Lastly, it is imperative that stakeholders realize the difference between an actionable plan and a hypothetical one. If you have a list of actions to be taken in the event of an attack or other tragedy, this is not a plan but a procedure, regardless of the amount of time that went into creating it or how many stakeholders you asked. It becomes a plan only once it is put to the test in the form of regular drills and simulations. Why? Because there is no such thing as a "typical" school day. Every day is different, as is every minute within each day.

Most schools will conduct drills at the most opportune time of the day, when all students are in a secure location and there is no lunch or other function like homecoming or prom activities, blood drives, pep rallies or assemblies going on. As these are the events that make up a great school experience, they are also perfect targets, which is why I submit that they are the perfect times to conduct a simulated attack; this is when we have the opportunities to find holes in the plan and mitigate those holes. This will undoubtedly save lives, especially when an event does actually happen in a more structured time—which they rarely do.

Awareness

As mentioned above, conducting real-life simulations and drills is necessary for constructing actionable plans. In addition to this, each individual must develop within themselves an awareness of the world around them. In police training, this is called situational awareness.

Everyone's situational awareness is different. We all see things through a different lens, but it is what manufactures those lenses that make the difference. For example, a person who has been through a major trauma, such as an assault—particularly one that was in an identifiable and often visited area—would probably have extremely acute situational awareness senses.

I break the quality of one's situational awareness into three types: Education, Perception, and Vision. Education, in the context of situational awareness, is framed by one's experiences and the way they understand, analyze, and departmentalize information as they encounter it.

For example, a teacher with a vast amount of classroom experience has great knowledge of the workings of classroom doors, windows, desks, chairs, and so on; thus, they can analyze the inner workings of this system within seconds. Once he or she walks into the hall, however, they encounter other children, other teachers, exit doors, hallways, et cetera, all of which are familiar but not departmentalized into sectors that allow them to question the norm. In this area, his or her senses would be regarded as "normal."

At Parkland High School, Nikolas Cruz was seen entering the school by at least two staff members. He was no longer a student. However, the fact that he had been a student and was familiar in that setting prevented the alarm bells from going off in the staff members' heads. They compartmentalized his presence as something that someone else could deal with, whether he was going to the office or to see another student, or any number of other reasonable explanations for him being there. The fact of the matter was that the monitors had been charged with securing a perimeter that they were not educated on through experiences or training, and therefore they failed to act when the norm was breached. This lack of awareness of the possible scenarios was a contributing factor to the several deaths that occurred that day.

The next area is how a human perceives evidence of normalcy. Normalcy is completely subjective, based solely on the perception of the researcher. You receive input through your senses, such as seeing the perpetrator or intruder in the hallway, smelling burned gunpowder, hearing gunfire, touching a weapon while restraining a student, or even tasting something that tainted the water supply. These senses, coupled with previous events that have occurred, are compounding and compelling evidence of a crisis situation. However, because one's perception is directly correlated to his or her experiences, the question becomes, would a normal human realize that a person who appeared to be a student was actually an intruder when there are hundreds of students in the school?

What if the teacher was a substitute? What if...? We can go on and on. What if the teacher had never smelled smoke from a weapon firing? What if the teacher had never heard gunfire, especially in a closed area like a school hallway where the sound reverberates through the hallways and corridors? What if the teacher thought the gunfire was construction workers, like Sandy Hook teachers did? What if they thought the gunfire was lockers slamming, like Marshall County students did? What if they thought the gunfire was actually balloons popping, as was reported after the Heath High School shooting? We can assume that we have all heard balloons popping and even lockers slamming at one point or another, so the norm would automatically gear towards what we have experienced, what we know and understand.

To have true awareness about what is actually happening, one must be willing to question and research as a matter of course. The scientific method must be incorporated on a daily basis, thereby expanding what we are comfortable knowing as well as our capacity for allowing additional data sets to affect our perception.

Vision, or the ability to predict possible future events and plan accordingly, is another critical component of situational awareness. Using the Logic Model, if a teacher had his/her children on the playground, and an event occurred, how could we help the children survive? What area is the event most likely to begin? The entrance? The trees? The road? Yes, the road is where the incident unfolded in Arkansas, where a fourteen-year-old killed his father, stole his truck and handgun, then crashed through the fence of an elementary school playground and started shooting. One child lost his life, but the quick action of the teachers saved countless others.

Presumably, every elementary school in the nation has some type of outdoor play area, yet such school systems rarely if ever take the time to create a mental vision of what a perpetrator might find appealing. This does not only apply to school systems; envisioning worst-case scenarios when we walk into a movie theater or Walmart will help sharpen our "futuring" skills so that walking into an area that is even possibly considered "familiar" to most will always be considered a learning opportunity to drive our situational awareness skills to the next level. To those who argue that this is a dismal view of the world, I would point out that this is the world we currently live in, and taking a dismal view is preferable to losing lives.

Responsiveness

In the last three decades, companies, law enforcement, and consulting firms have put forth a great deal of effort to come up with the "best" ways to respond to crises. This was based on their research and, in some cases, experience of crises. None of this research, however, has concluded that one type of response is the best in keeping kids safe. What does this mean? We must rely on our awareness to note and respond to even the most minor breaches in the norm—the norm that you have calculated with your perceptions of regularity.

When the sheriff of Marshall County, Kentucky stated that the kids did "exactly as they were trained to do," he basically used his knowledge of the event to justify a response to the crisis. Where was the response when the child was having thoughts of suicide? Where was the response when the child was standing alone?

The normalcy of childhood is a fallacy. There is nothing normal in experiences when a child is growing and learning from the environment, and we as schools are an active part of providing that environment. That said, a child spends approximately 12% of their time annually in a school. That means almost 88% of their lives are being influenced by non-school events and occurrences that shape their frame of mind and mold their senses into the person that they become. This begs the question, how can we best influence children in such a small amount of time? By teaching other children, parents, and community members who interact in that world to first and foremost respond to challenged children and to respond to a breach in the norm.

Technology, particularly social media, presents both opportunities and challenges in this area. In creating their online personas, children are grasping for their true identity—for their "why." Odd or even disturbing behavior online has become so commonplace that it is often considered "normal," attention-grabbing or possibly a "well that's just how Johnny is" type of analysis from the masses. It is a travesty that in the wealthiest nation in the world, a child must wait for a school to get resources to help them grow and learn. It is unconscionable that society believes schools should be the social catch-all when responding to mental anguish, to homelessness, to poverty, and to violence when the response should come from the 88%. It truly takes a village, and much of that village is falling down on the job.

Advocacy

The final and possibly most important component of the PARA Method to School Safety concerns the cohesiveness schools have had within their communities since the early settler days. Since the overwhelming amount of violence in schools occurs at the secondary level, let's focus on where we need to go from where we have been. The first public high schools in the U.S. opened in Boston in 1821. Since then, what has changed in the way we organize and interpret learning and interaction?

In 1821, classrooms were set with multiple rows of desks facing forward and a teacher at the head of the classroom; it is largely the same today. In 1821, students were allowed unstructured time to go to their lockers and for lunch to interact with other children. The same is true today. In 1821, students received an education that society believed they should receive in order to be considered a "productive citizen." The same is true in the present day, albeit with far more state mandates for learning.

Children are different today only because their experiences in the other 88% of their lives are vastly different. Why are we still molding them and attempting to make them acquiesce to a setting that is more for control than learning? It is a setting that is beautiful architecture with herding qualities to maintain order in movement—a setting that was possibly positive and nurturing in 1821 but is not so today.

If we are truly in need of some type of transformational change, why are legislators ignoring their responsibility as representatives of the 88%? Why are people maintaining comfort instead of conforming to the present needs of kids and families? Because our advocacy efforts are not focused on forward-thinking grassroots endeavors but on putting out fires.

Why is it that some schools are still unlocked to the public during times in which children are present and accessible? Why are some systems oblivious to obvious breaches in the normalcy of learning and chalk it up to the performance of the 12%?

It is time we crawl out of our comfortable shells and each teacher, parent, community member, business owner, law enforcement officer and clergy member take a stand in their daily routines to point out and submit research on individualized "norms" rather than that of the herd. It is time that teaching and learning in a nurturing environment involves individualized education plans on all children, not just special education students. And it is certainly time we increase the culpability of the 88% and its longstanding effect on the safety of our children when they attend school.

How, then, does PARA play out in the real world? The first step is to build a team comprised of a variety of those stakeholders mentioned above so that different viewpoints are represented. That said, the team should have one leader, preferably a school administrator or even a school counselor or social worker. The team will be responsible for creating a comprehensive threat assessment and management plan that includes both threats from individual students (Behavior Threat Assessments) and protecting the physical building. I have worked within my district, region, and certainly the state to foster relationships with government representatives, law enforcement, parents, public health agencies, medical providers and more. Education is not just for children. Those of us with the capacity to inform change have an obligation to do so.

We have covered in previous chapters what this team can do in terms of becoming aware of a troubled and potentially violent student—the "front lines" if you will. Here, we address threats caused by the facility itself. Perimeter doors should be locked at all times. Those the school chooses to keep unlocked must have another system in place to monitor and control entry and exit and communicate with the systems in place. Ideally, lock and key systems should be replaced with heavy-duty magnetic locks and card readers that not only control entry but record who has come into the school. In schools that keep the lock and key systems, latch guards should be installed to reduce the chance of forcible entry. Master keys that allow access to all areas should be limited to staff who absolutely need it.

Surveillance systems with real-time mobile access should be in place throughout the school and grounds, along with alarm systems that are connected to and monitored by local law enforcement as well as school administrators. Staff should be thoroughly and continually trained on both systems.

Staff should also be trained and frequently drilled on the content of the formal security plan. This plan should encompass, among other things:

- Security and surveillance in the parking lots

- Staff, student and visitor identification protocols

- Security training for all staff, including maintenance and cafeteria staff as well as substitute teachers

- Training in the safe handling of mail

- Detailed and emergency lockdown procedures and mandatory regular drilling of these measures

- Standardized information collection and evaluation protocols—this falls under the heading of threat awareness and includes strategies around enlisting other students to report troubling behavior and investigating these reports immediately.

As mentioned earlier, PARA is not a one-size-fits-all approach; each state, district, or region must examine its particular set of challenges and resources at its disposal. For example, a solution that works in an urban area will not necessarily work in a suburban or rural one, and vice versa. Why is this? The primary difference between rural and urban settings is the probability of violence. In other words, the statistical probabilities are greater or lesser depending on the size of the population, both within a school's walls and the surrounding macro-system.

Gang violence is vicious and pervasive in some areas, yet we must remember that just because a child joins a gang does not necessarily mean they are violent. Those who have chosen a life working in public education are charged with teaching children, in most cases for approximately seven hours per day and a general 180 days per year. That means we are spending 1,260 hours out of a possible 8,760 hours per year with them. Remember, although that sounds like a lot, it is only 12% of their time; the rest is spent outside the school safety net.

In rural America, where the macro-system population is sparse, the simple interaction with other individuals during non-school time is proportionately less and presumably less of an opportunity to see a "turf" issue on a geographic area like you would see in a heavily populated area. That is not to say rural schools are not dangerous, for they face greater threats due to cultural complacency and lack of prioritized resources, but they generally do have smaller schools that promote better "connectedness" with their students. A PARA-compliant plan must be created with these differences in mind and also allowing for the structure of individual schools.

For example, rural schools must fight complacency with well-thought-out priorities for keeping kids safe. Simply because it hasn't happened in your school or even not typically in rural schools does not mean it can't or won't, and you should be prepared.

In urban areas, schools need to have fewer students and more space. While this is a tall order in cities with denser populations and presumably very limited space on which to build, the reality is that a feeling of confinement within ecosystems provides a stressor for kids that will actually prevent connectedness. Students in such schools tend to get lost in a large system rather than finding the very people who truly care about them—their teachers.

When discussing PARA, I am inevitably asked about the efficacy and safety of arming teachers and/or other school staff. This has come to the forefront in the past few years and, given the current political polarization in this country, is a hotly contested debate. It is also a necessary one. With the exceptions of Columbine, which took sixteen minutes, and the second Virginia Tech attack, which took about ten minutes, most school shootings are over in four to five minutes. The average response time for law enforcement: 7.77 minutes. Taken together, these facts tell us that once the shooting starts, we cannot rely solely on law enforcement. They also tell us that if we are diligent in our efforts, we can prevent at least a good portion of them.

It is not my intention to get mired in politics. However, given the topic of this book, I would be remiss if I did not weigh in on this issue based on my experience in law enforcement and as a school resource officer.

While there is no empirical evidence of the best response, there is no denying that as administrators of schools and other potential targets in a confined area, we must create and implement protocols that allow us to delay or inhibit an armed intruder until law enforcement can arrive. What we are really saying is that we are in a "holding pattern" in attempting to provide a barrier to a gun or other weapon-wielding intruder until someone with a superior weapon arrives. Having an armed person or persons already at the school would certainly decrease the amount of time that elapses between contact with the armed assailant and the mitigation or end of that threat.

That said, simply having armed personnel does not always equal instant safety for kids, as illustrated by the 1999 shooting at Columbine. In that case, there was an armed law enforcement officer on school grounds, but he had neither the training nor the superior firepower to be able to mitigate the situation due to several factors, including but not limited to: the fact that there were two assailants to one officer; the assailants had weapons with larger capacity magazines and therefore could cover a great deal of ground—and fire off a lot more rounds—before needing to reload; the officer, and most officers during that time period, was trained (if at all) to engage using a team of officers (i.e., in a "diamond formation"); this lack of training meant that he remained outside the building and was essentially prevented from taking action until special forces arrived.

This issue again came to the forefront after the Parkland shooting when Officer Scot Peterson came under fire both legally and in the media for not entering the school. Peterson, who had an exemplary record before the incident, was called a coward and placed on unpaid leave. Reasonable minds can disagree on his culpability, but one thing is clear: firepower, without the proper tactical training and the proper protocols for backup in place, is not only ineffective, but it can also be deadly.

Given these situations, what can schools and/or law

enforcement agencies do to make schools safer? Teachers are, by their very job description, there to protect their students, not run toward gunfire. To place that burden on their shoulders is unrealistic and irresponsible. Teachers are not going to leave their children in their classrooms to confront somebody who is firing a gun in or around the building.

What if they leave and the perpetrator comes into their classroom and inflicts harm on those children? In addition, the shooter likely has a better weapon—possibly a rifle with a thirty-round magazine—while most concealed carry firearms are .380 caliber, 9-millimeter, or a .45 with a six-round magazine. Sending a mildly trained individual with limited firepower to a gunfight is suicide.

Some states allow teachers who possess a concealed carry permit to carry on school premises. This could potentially mitigate the multiple aggressor threat so long as the teacher(s) have similar or powerful weapons. However, there are many issues associated with this, and, once again, finances, training, and clear responsibility are at the forefront. Some schools found that their current insurance companies refused to cover them if they allowed teachers to carry weapons. Thus, they would have to foot the bill for supplemental insurance. This would be cost prohibitive for many poor school districts that are already struggling to meet the everyday expenses of educating their students.

And what of the federal government? Currently, it spends less than 2% of the entire national budget on education but billions on securing government buildings. As schools are subject to federal mandates (i.e., standardized test scores) that affect their funding, they should also be treated as government facilities to receive adequate funding for security. This means, at the very least, that the government should pay for a highly trained law enforcement officer to be in every single school in America. Then we will have secured our schools with a person that's concentrating solely on protecting our children. We already have a great, untapped resource—former military or correctional officers who are already highly trained in security. We need a federal law that allows schools to utilize these people, along with highly trained law enforcement officers, so that we as a nation can finally list "protecting our future generations" as our greatest achievement.

In the absence of such a federal statute, several states have enacted laws allowing different types of people who have been trained in security to be in schools, but like many politically charged issues, it is not uniform across the nation. States with those laws, and assuming they can afford it, might opt to use those dollars for a specially-trained law enforcement officer, which also has its pros and cons.

What do I mean when I use the term "specially trained"? In most states, law enforcement officers must qualify, on an annual basis, with their duty weapon and any other weapon they might use in the course of their job. Many states do not require this type of intensive training for concealed carry permit holders. Law enforcement officers also receive training around multiple-officer and multiple-agency response and how to counter when there are other officers on the scene. Again, civilian concealed carry holders only receive a static distance qualifying practice. More specifically, and to address the training that was an issue with the 1999 Columbine incident, law enforcement officers can receive training on solo engagement specifically for school-based response to an active threat.

The ALICE Institute provides a training called RAIDER (Rapid Deployment, Awareness, Intervention, Decisiveness, EMS, and Recovery), which is only school and classroom-based and instructs law enforcement on engaging threats by both students and adults in a school setting. This is for law enforcement only, so concealed carry holders—even those employed by a school—would not be allowed in the training. Lastly, many law enforcement departments have come to understand the value in providing their officers with extended capacity weapons and extensive training with them as an effective means of matching or overpowering assailants. As concealed carry holders are not permitted to possess such weapons, and small-caliber concealed weapons are little match for a high capacity, high-powered rifle or other assault weapons, the challenge of "fighting fire with fire" remains.

In general, I am certainly in favor of having weapons at schools, including and especially high-capacity, high-powered weapons that will match anything an individual could purchase at a local gun store, gun fair or other venue. However, I am not, for the reasons noted above, in favor of concealed carry permit holders to be those persons, at least not in the sense that we would rely upon them to mitigate a threat.

Without some type of specific training, similar to ALICE, having teachers or other staff bringing a weapon to school could be more dangerous on a day-to-day basis than the threat of an armed intruder. That said, having at least one individual within the school who is licensed to carry a weapon and who can be trained as a school security personnel and be at least annually trained and licensed to carry multiple weapons may be the answer. That, as described, is a law enforcement officer. Schools can work with their local municipality to authorize such an individual, but it takes cooperation across agencies and an intergovernmental agreement that specifically designates duties while working as school personnel (teacher, custodian, administrator, etc.) and duties as a trained law enforcement officer.

As mentioned in previous chapters, guns are not the problem but merely a tool of someone who, for a myriad of reasons, decides to kill his/her fellow students, teachers, and administrators. Individuals who possess guns can enter any school in the nation—IF the schools are not protected by equal firepower AND manpower.

Simply having a law enforcement officer on campus is not the answer to being safe. Students were hurt, some fatally, at Columbine High School, Marshall County High School, Stoneman-Douglas High School, etc., and they had a trained officer with weapons on campus.

Laws permitting access to guns do not make schools any more dangerous; the danger exists because we do not build them or typically staff them to keep people with weapons out. It is similar to the so-called "war on drugs."

Has making their possession and use illegal stopped those who want to acquire them from doing so? Hardly. Instead, it has created a criminal underworld while at the same time incarcerating countless people for the "crime" of being addicted.

If guns were illegal, that would not stop those who want them from acquiring them. What should be illegal is not recognizing the fact that our nation's kids and their teachers are targets for extremists and our reluctance around providing the necessary resources to our schools to keep them safe.

Employing a school-based trained law enforcement officer or, better yet, multiple officers, should be as important as reading and math. It should certainly be more important than fighting amongst ourselves about whether the weapon used by a school shooter should have been illegal. Someone as motivated as Adam Lanza or Nikolas Cruz would have found another way to inflict the pain and suffering on their perceived enemies and to garner the media attention they felt they so richly deserved.

CONCLUSION

"Complacency is a disease—the PARA mindset is the cure."
—*Steve Webb, Ph.D.*

As I was completing this book, the country was rocked by the suicides of Jeremy Richman—a parent of one of the Sandy Hook Elementary School victims—and Calvin Desir and Sydney Aiello, both of whom were students at Marjory Douglas Stoneman High School. Though they came from different walks of life, each had been destroyed by a school massacre. Reading these heartbreaking accounts, it was never more apparent to me the far-reaching effects of school violence; not just on the students and teachers who are present during the event but our entire society.

By all accounts, Jeremy Richman was channeling his grief into positive action. After his six-year-old daughter Arielle was killed by Adam Lanza in December of 2012, he—along with his wife, Jennifer Hensel—founded the Arielle Foundation; the purpose of which is to research brain abnormalities that have been connected to violent behavior. He even left his job at a pharmaceutical company in order to devote more time to building his daughter's legacy. His mission was to change the world through compassion, and he seemed excited about that mission right up until the day his body was found.

Richman's suicide shocked everyone who knew him, from his closest family, friends, and colleagues to the police officers who responded to the call—some of whom were also called out to Sandy Hook on the day of the shooting.

The two other suicides: sixteen-year-old Calvin Desir and nineteen-year-old Sydney Aiello, had both attended Marjory Douglas Stoneman at the time of the shooting. According to Aiello's family, Sydney, who had lost close friends at the hands of Nikolas Cruz, suffered from PTSD and survivor's guilt. It is not clear whether anyone knew of Desir's distress, only that he, like Aiello, ended his life with a gunshot.

Their deaths, which all occurred within a week in March of 2019, tell us that the carnage does not end with the incident, or the investigation, or the media coverage; it fans out far into the future, forever altering, and oftentimes stealing, the potential of those left behind. In other words, surviving the shooting does not necessarily make one a "survivor."

Throughout this book, we have discussed the multifaceted challenges we face around educating and protecting our children—from the cookie-cutter mentality of standardized tests to the overprescribing of pharmaceuticals, from cyberbullying to gun violence. Reasonable minds can disagree about which of these factors poses the greatest threat, but the fact remains that the only way to fix our broken system is not to prioritize one issue or another, and it is certainly not to engage in political posturing and winner-takes-all battles. Stakeholders must be willing to cross the aisle and to utilize a comprehensive plan that focuses on forming a network that supports children on the physical, emotional, and academic levels.

This network includes understanding students on an individualized level, not just as scores on a standardized test. It means acknowledging that one size does not fit all; not every child wants to, or is cut out to, go to college no matter how much pressure we place on them or how much Adderall we prescribe.

We also must be willing to think outside the box when it comes to socialization. This means broadening our minds to understand that social media is not simply a passing thing to be managed but is a permanent part of our world that can and must be utilized as a tool. It also means acknowledging that for some kids gaming can be as community-building as being part of a sports team.

Most importantly, it means doing everything we can to make every child feel seen and special and necessary so that they do not crave the attention and notoriety of countless people on Facebook, Snapchat or Twitter, and certainly not for committing some heinous act in order to get that needed attention. No one would want to emulate a Nikolas Cruz or Adam Lanza. The Cynosure Effect, at least with respect to our kids, would dramatically decrease.

The PARA Mindset achieves this. More importantly, it trains us to break free of the culture of complacency and start behaving as if the future of our society depends on fixing these problems ... because it does.

About the Author

Dr. Steven Webb is an award-winning educator, school resource officer, and the founder of Safe School Systems, LLC, a consulting firm that helps schools and communities enact and enhance common-sense school safety tactics.

He is a nationally known school safety expert who has been recognized by the National School Public Relations Association (IL) with the Distinguished Service Award of Excellence and named a "Leader Among Us" by the Southern Business Journal.

Dr. Webb has been President of both the Illinois Association of School Administrators and the Association of Illinois Rural and Small Schools. He is currently a member of the American Association of School Administrators Governing Board, the Illinois Terrorism Task Force School Safety Commission, and the Illinois Department of Child and Family Services Child Death Review Board.

Dr. Webb is a certified A.L.I.C.E. Active Threat Training Instructor and R.A.I.D.E.R. Solo Engagement Tactics Level II Instructor for law enforcement. He is also an Associate Professor in Educational Administration at Southern Illinois University and McKendree University, specializing in school law and policy.